STU

AS Physical Education

UNIT 3

Edexcel

Unit 3: Exercise and Training

Philip Allan Updates
Market Place
Deddington
Oxfordshire
OX15 0SE

tel: 01869 338652
fax: 01869 337590
e-mail: sales@philipallan.co.uk
www.philipallan.co.uk

© Philip Allan Updates 2005

ISBN-13: 978-1-84489-029-3
ISBN-10: 1-84489-029-5

All rights reserved; no part of this publication may be reproduced, stored in a retrieval system, or transmitted, in any form or by any means, electronic, mechanical, photocopying, recording or otherwise without either the prior written permission of Philip Allan Updates or a licence permitting restricted copying in the United Kingdom issued by the Copyright Licensing Agency Ltd, 90 Tottenham Court Road, London W1T 4LP.

This Guide has been written specifically to support students preparing for the Edexcel AS Physical Education Unit 3 examination. The content has been neither approved nor endorsed by Edexcel and remains the sole responsibility of the author.

Printed by MPG Books, Bodmin

Environmental information
The paper on which this title is printed is sourced from managed, sustainable forests.

P00538

Contents

Introduction

About this guide

This guide is written to help you prepare for Unit Test 3, which examines the content of **Unit 3: Exercise & Training**. This unit investigates the fundamental principles needed to ensure that training has the desired effect, namely to improve performance. It examines the structural and functional responses and adaptations in the body that enable these improvements to take place. There are three sections to the guide:

- **Introduction** — this provides advice on how to use the guide, an explanation of the skills required in AS PE and suggestions for effective revision. It offers guidance on how to apply your knowledge in the examination.
- **Content Guidance** — this section summarises the specification content of Unit 3.
- **Questions and Answers** — this contains four mock questions for you to try. Each question has been attempted by two candidates, Candidate A and Candidate B. Their answers, along with the examiner's comments, should help you to see what you need to do to achieve a good grade — and how you can easily *miss* marks even though you may understand the topic.

How should I use this guide?

This guide can be used throughout your physical education course — it is not *just* a revision aid. Because the Content Guidance is laid out in sections that correspond to those of the specification for Unit 3, you can use it:

- to check that your notes cover the material required by the specification
- to identify strengths and weaknesses
- as a reference for homework and internal tests
- during your revision to prepare 'bite-sized' chunks of related material, rather than being faced with a file full of notes

The Questions and Answers section can be used to:

- identify the terms used by examiners in questions and what they expect of you
- familiarise yourself with the style of questions you can expect
- identify the ways in which marks are lost as well as the ways in which they are gained

The specification

To make a good start to studying Unit 3, it is important that you have access to the specification. Your teacher should have a copy, or you can obtain your own from the awarding body at **www.edexcel.org.uk**.

The specification identifies everything that needs to be covered and understood. If a topic is in the specification, then it could be examined; if it is not, it will not be examined.

On reading the specification, you might assume that the first three sections concern anatomy and physiology and that the final two concern training. However, it would be a mistake to approach the unit in this way. All the sections should be looked at from the perspective of an athlete. For example, when learning anatomy, it should be tackled in terms of:

> 'this type of training for this body part will produce this response and adaptation, so that performance will be affected in the following way...'

Key terms

It is essential that you are familiar with the following terms:

- **anatomy** — the physical structure of the body
- **physiology** — the way the body functions
- **response** — a temporary change that happens quickly
- **adaptation** — a permanent change that takes place over time
- **structural** — describes make-up or anatomy and often relates to a change
- **functional** — describes the way the body works (its physiology) and often relates to a change

Activity

Arrange the items in this list into an 'order of events' and then provide an example for each item:

- adaptations
- physiology
- stress
- responses
- functional responses
- types of stress
- anatomy
- structural responses
- structural adaptations
- functional adaptations

It may be helpful to picture the body as a clever but lazy combination of parts, to the extent that it constantly seeks out ways to function with the least amount of effort. Consequently, responses take place that enable the body to function with minimal effort and adaptations occur to enable the body to perform in a now familiar environment without undue stress. For example, adaptations that enable an aerobic athlete to perform better occur so that the body meets the demands made on it with less stress.

Study skills and revision strategies

Revision and preparation for examinations are very personal. However, there are common approaches that should be employed by all. Being successful in any subject is dependent upon:

- understanding — the ability to follow a particular concept
- learning — the ability to recall the concept without prompts
- application — the ability to use the knowledge you have learnt to answer the questions that have been asked

The Questions and Answers section of this guide deals with application.

Past papers can be very useful. They will familiarise you with the format of the questions and the language used. There are also mark schemes and examiners' reports available. These indicate the sorts of mistakes made by students when faced with particular questions. They also include some model answers.

There are several ways of learning and individuals will have particular favourites determined by their preferred learning style(s), whether it is auditory, visual or kinaesthetic. However, there are common areas of good practice that should be adopted by all students. Whatever your preferred style, you must work out a revision plan.

What you must do

- Leave yourself enough time to cover all the material identified in the Unit 3 specification.
- Make sure that you actually have all the material to hand (use this book as a basis).
- Identify weaknesses early in your preparation so that you have time to do something about them.
- Familiarise yourself with the terminology used in the examination questions (see page 7).

What you *could* do to help you learn

- Copy selected sections of your notes.
- Summarise your notes into a more compact format, including the key points.
- Create your own flash cards — write key points on postcards (carry them around with you for quick revision during coffee breaks or on the bus).
- Make audio recordings of your notes and/or the key points and play these back.
- Make a PowerPoint presentation of the key points and use this to revise in the last few days before the unit test.
- Discuss a topic with a friend who is studying the same course.
- Try to explain a topic to someone who is *not* following the course.
- Practise examination questions on a topic.

Approaching the unit test

Terms used in examination questions

You will be asked precise questions in the examination, so you can save a lot of valuable time — as well as ensuring you score as many marks as possible — by knowing what is expected. Terms most commonly used are explained below.

Brief

This means that only a short statement of the main points is required.

Define

This requires you to state the meaning of a term, without using the term itself.

Describe

This is a request for factual detail about a structure or process, expressed logically and concisely, without explanation.

Discuss

You are required to give a critical account of various viewpoints and arguments on the topic set, drawing attention to their relative importance and significance.

Evaluate

This means that a judgement of evidence and/or arguments is required.

Explain

This means that reasons have to be included in your answer.

Identify

This requires a word, phrase or brief statement to show that you recognise a concept or theory in an item.

List

This requires a sequence of numbered points, one below the other, with no further explanation.

Outline

This means give only the main points, i.e. don't go into detail. Don't be tempted to write more than necessary — this will waste time.

State

A brief, concise answer, without reasons, is required.

Suggest

This means that the question has no fixed answer and a wide range of reasonable responses is acceptable.

What is meant by...?

This usually requires a definition. The amount of information needed is indicated by the mark allocation.

The unit test

When you finally open the test paper, it can be quite a stressful moment. However, remember that you have a lot of choice — there are four questions, of which you have to answer two. Making the right choice is very important. Read all the questions carefully before deciding which to attempt. Other strategies include the following:

- *Do not* begin to write as soon as you open the paper.
- *Do* scan *all* the questions on the paper before you start your answers.
- *Do* identify those questions about which you feel most confident and answer these first regardless of their position on the paper.
- *Do* read the question carefully — if you are asked to explain, then explain, don't just describe.
- *Do* take notice of the mark allocation and try to match this in terms of the number of points you make in your answer.
- *Do* try to stick to the point in your answer (it is easy to stray into related areas that will not score marks and will use up valuable time).
- *Make sure* you fulfil the examination rubric, i.e. answer the correct number of questions from each section.

Time allocation

Do not waste time writing material that will not score marks. Take the following example:

Outline the reasons why an athlete would warm up prior to exercise. (2 marks)

This is a straightforward question. When it appeared in an examination paper, most students scored the full 2 marks. Many students scored those marks in a couple of sentences and then wasted time writing another half page. Remember, 2 marks means you have to make just two points.

Break the question down

Ask yourself: 'How many things am I being asked to do?' Identify the different parts of the question to ensure that you do everything asked, therefore making it possible to gain all the available marks. Take the following example:

Identify and explain the stages of a warm up for a sport of your choice. (6 marks)

This question has 3 marks available for the first part of the question — *identifying* the stages of a warm up — and 3 marks for the second part of the question — *explaining* the stages of a warm up.

Plan your answer

Try to be concise, but make sure that you include enough points to match the marks available. Take the following example:

Identify three responses to exercise. Explain why each response occurs and state its benefit for the performer. (9 marks)

This question asks you to:

- identify
- explain why
- state the benefit

It would be easy to write a mini-essay that contains a lot of detailed sports science, but fails to answer one or more parts of the question. The question asks for three things, three times. By structuring your answer, you should be able to identify nine points:

- first response
- explain why this response occurs
- state the benefit of this response
- second response
- explain why the second response occurs...and so on

Answer the question set

It is very important to answer the question set and not one that you wish had been set. Take the following example:

Identify the adaptations to, and benefits for, the muscular system that result from aerobic training. (3 marks)

Answers relating to the cardiovascular or skeletal systems will only serve to waste time and will not score any marks.

Content Guidance

This section is a guide to the content of **Unit 3: Exercise and Training**. The main areas covered are:

- immediate effects of exercise
- musculo-skeletal structures in action
- circulatory, vascular and respiratory (CVR) systems in action
- measurement and evaluation of fitness components
- planning of fitness and training programmes

You may already be familiar with some of the information in these topic areas. However, it is important that you know and understand this information exactly as described in the specification. This summary of the specification content highlights key points and you should find it useful when revising for the Unit 3 test.

Immediate effects of exercise

Key points

- Reasons for warming up and cooling down.
- How to warm up and cool down.
- The responses that occur during warm-up and cool-down.
- Different ways of stretching and their suitability for different activities.

You should be able to describe the process of warming up for:

- an endurance athlete
- a power athlete
- your chosen sport

Warm-up

Warm-up has become a generic term for the activities performed in preparation for exercise. As such, its most fundamental objectives are to prepare the athlete fully, both mentally and physically. The athlete should, therefore, enjoy an improved performance and the likelihood of injury should be reduced.

The body functions optimally at a specific temperature and during the warm-up both core and localised temperatures increase. Extremes of temperature affect performance adversely, so during the warm-up the body begins to employ a more efficient system of temperature regulation.

As many of the physiological aspects of a warm-up as possible should be specific to the activity about to be performed. For example, if a ball is used in the activity, then a ball should be incorporated into the warm-up. This makes it possible to see how neuromuscular aspects could be improved.

Stages of warm-up

Stage 1: initial preparation

The aim is to encourage the necessary responses to facilitate improved performance. This is achieved through gross motor skills, using slow, continuous exercise, and increasing in intensity.

The benefits include:

- the release of adrenaline, which results in an increase in heart rate
- increased ventilation, which speeds up oxygen delivery
- heat generation
- speeding up localised muscular metabolism
- dilation of blood vessels
- increased muscle elasticity, which results in greater force and speed of contraction
- decreased muscle viscosity, which results in greater force and speed of contraction, and greater flexibility

Stage 2: injury prevention

The aim is to minimise the risk of injury. This is achieved through stretching — active static, passive static, ballistic, dynamic and proprioceptor neuromuscular facilitation (PNF).

The benefits include:

- reduced risk of injury
- an improvement in tension/tone over a greater length of the muscle, enabling a greater force to be exerted
- a reduction in loss of performance with age
- postural improvements

Stage 3: skill practice

The aim is to strengthen the link between mind and muscle and to improve confidence. This is achieved through practising with a partner or group.

The benefits include:

- improved reaction and response due to the increased frequency of nerve impulses
- improved timing, which minimises the risk of injury

Stage 4: sport specific

This is the final preparation before the performance. It is achieved through practising with a partner or group, with increased intensity and simulation of performance conditions.

The benefits are that:

- confidence is developed
- performance is aided

Cool-down

The warm-up prepares for activity; the cool-down prepares for inactivity and for the next training session.

By gradually reducing the intensity of the activity over a period of approximately 20 minutes, the body is able to start the process of recovery more effectively and quickly.

Cool-down involves performing light, continuous exercise during which the heart rate remains elevated. The purpose is to keep metabolic activity high and blood vessels dilated so that oxygen can be flushed through the muscle tissue, removing and oxidising any lactic acid that remains. This prevents blood pooling in the veins which, if exercise is stopped abruptly, can cause dizziness.

The final part of the cool-down period should involve a period of stretching exercises. It is only after recovery has been completed that future training should be considered.

THE HENLEY COLLEGE LIBRARY

Stretching

Stretching is certainly the best way of maintaining or improving muscle elasticity. Performing stretching during a cool-down is an excellent way of maintaining elasticity while aiding recovery.

The different modes of stretching are:

- static — the muscle is taken to its limit and held under tension
  - active static involves the performer stretching the body part
  - passive static is when the performer allows a partner to move the limb to the point of stretch
- ballistic — momentum is used to force the fibres to stretch over a greater range
- PNF — the muscle is stretched to its limit and then undergoes an isometric contraction while stretched; the muscle is relaxed and the process is repeated
- dynamic — the muscle is stretched through a range of movements

The value of pre-activity stretching is currently topical. Performing static stretching in preparation for more sport-specific stretching in a warm-up is almost certainly good practice. However, what is considered dubious is carrying out a few static stretches before embarking upon a particularly ballistic activity, such as trampolining or high hurdling.

Musculo-skeletal structures in action

Key points

- Different types of skeletal muscle fibre and their suitability to athletic activities.
- Different types of joint and supporting structures and their roles in sporting movements.
- Types of contraction/muscle action and the differing roles played by muscles.
- How the musculo-skeletal system works to produce movement.

You should be able to analyse movement.

Background

- Muscles are attached to bones by **tendons**.
- At joints, bones are attached to bones by **ligaments**.
- Cartilage assists at joints.
- Muscles can only contract, but there are different types of contraction and muscles can take on several different roles.
- Muscle contraction gives stability, allows movement and produces heat.

All muscles have at least one point of **origin** (where they are anchored to the skeleton) and one point of **insertion**. When a muscle contracts, it pulls on the point(s) of insertion and the bone is pulled towards the point of origin. This happens because muscles are attached to bones by tendons. An example is shown in the diagram below.

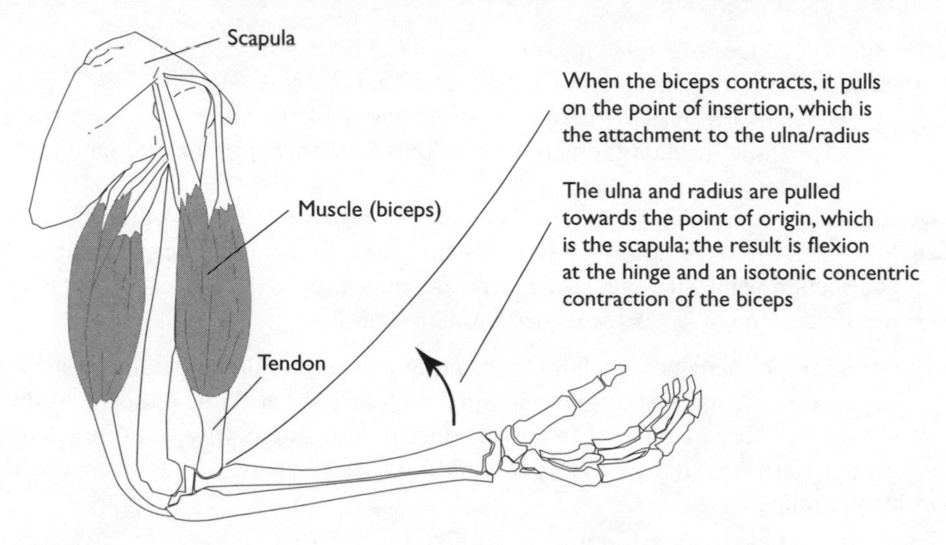

The amount of movement possible is determined by the joint structure and the elasticity of the muscle. Combined, these produce **flexibility**.

Types of muscular contraction

Muscles can perform different types of contraction:

- In **isotonic contraction**, movement occurs. This can take the form of:
  - isotonic **concentric** contraction — the muscle actively shortens. This process usually works in opposition to gravity — for example, lifting a weight in a biceps curl.
  - isotonic **eccentric** contraction — the muscle lengthens, generally working as a brake or to slow down a movement. This process usually occurs in the direction of gravity — for example, lowering a weight in a biceps curl.
- In **isometric contraction**, a force exerted by a muscle meets an equal resistance and no movement occurs.
- In **isokinetic contraction**, the speed and/or force of contraction is consistent throughout the range of motion.

Muscles have various roles:

- **agonist** — an active muscle at an active joint
- **antagonist** — a passive muscle at an active joint
- **prime mover** — the main contributing agonist
- **fixator** — a stabiliser at the point of origin
- **synergist** — a stabiliser at the point of insertion or elsewhere in the body

Gross muscle structure

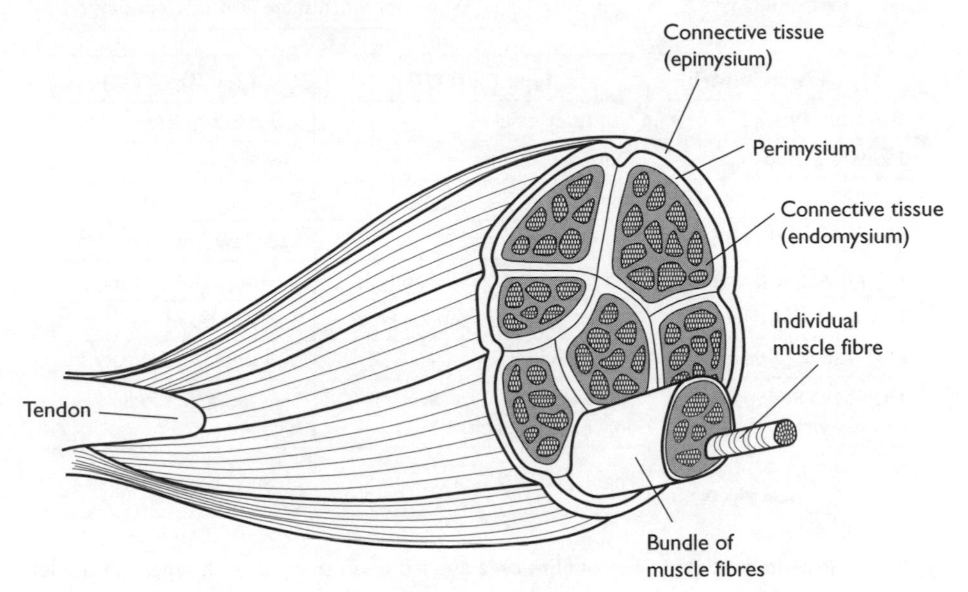

Generally a muscle consists of a '**belly**', with a fibrous tendon for attachment to the bone and an outer protective layer called the **epimysium**.

The muscle belly is made up of a collection of bundles called **fascicles**. Each fascicle has a protective sheath called the **perimysium** and consists of many **fibres**, or **muscle cells**, gathered together in a bunch. These fibres contain numerous **myofibrils**, which run parallel to each other and extend the entire length of the muscle fibre. There may be hundreds of thousands of myofibrils within each single muscle fibre.

The myofibrils are the contractile element of the muscle. Each myofibril consists of even smaller contractile units called **sarcomeres**, giving rise to characteristic dark and light bands.

Types of skeletal muscle fibre

There are two basic fibre types: **slow twitch** and **fast twitch**. Fast-twitch fibres are subdivided into **type IIa** (**f**ast-twitch-**o**xidative-**g**lycolytic, FOG) and **type IIb** fibres (**f**ast-**t**witch-**g**lycolytic, FTG). Therefore, there are three groups — **type I** (slow twitch), and types IIa and IIb (both fast twitch).

Type I fibres work best with oxygen; type IIb fibres work best when there is insufficient oxygen. Fibres that work best with oxygen must have characteristics that enable them to do so. If fibres are trained for their specific design, then they become even better at working with or without oxygen. For example, when experiencing aerobic training, type IIb fibres will take on the characteristics of type IIa fibres, while type IIa fibres will take on the characteristics of type I fibres.

Work well with oxygen ⟷ Work well when there is insufficient oxygen

Type I (slow twitch)	Type IIa (FOG)	Type IIb (FTG)
Contract slowly	Contract quicker	Contract quickest
Moderately powerful	Quite powerful	Very powerful
Small	Bigger	Biggest
Lots of mitochondria	Fewer mitochondria	Very few mitochondria
High myoglobin content	Moderate myoglobin content	Low myoglobin content
Resistant to fatigue	Moderately resistant to fatigue	Easily fatigued
High capillary density	High capillary density	Low capillary density
High aerobic capacity; low anaerobic capacity	Relatively high aerobic and anaerobic capacity	Low aerobic capacity; high anaerobic capacity
Low energy stores (ATP, PC and muscle glycogen)	Higher energy stores	Highest energy stores

Tip **If you visualise the three types of fibre on a line from left to right, with type I on the left, type IIa in the middle and type IIb on the right, then all you have to remember is 'left is with O_2' and 'right is without O_2'.**

Adaptaions to exercise

All three types of fibre adapt to exercise, as summarised in the table below.

Exercise	Type I	Type IIa	Type IIb
Low-intensity, long-duration	Become better able to produce energy aerobically	Start to take on type I characteristics	Begin to become more aerobically efficient
High-intensity, short-duration, repeated with little rest	Take on type IIa characteristics	Become better able to delay lactic acid build-up	Take on type IIa characteristics
High-intensity, short-duration	Begin to become more anaerobically efficient	Start to take on type IIb characteristics	Become better able to produce energy anaerobically

Joints

Types of joint

An **articulation** or **joint** is where bones meet. There are three main types of joint, categorised according to the amount of movement each allows.

- **Synovial joints** allow the most movement. There are different types of synovial joint. For example, ball-and-socket joints are found at the shoulder and hip; hinge joints occur at the elbow and knee.
- **Cartilaginous joints**, such as the joints in the vertebral column, allow some restricted movement. Discs of cartilage help to absorb shock and also permit some movement.

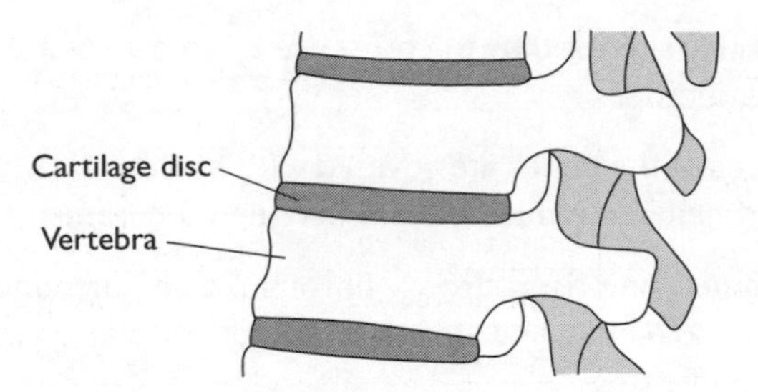

- **Fibrous joints**, such as the sutures that fuse the cranial bones together, allow very little (if any) movement. The joints are clearly visible, but the strength of the connective tissue holds them in place.

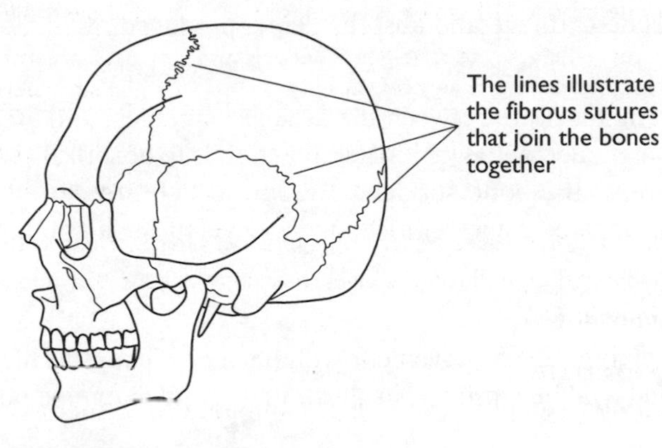

Structures and features of synovial joints

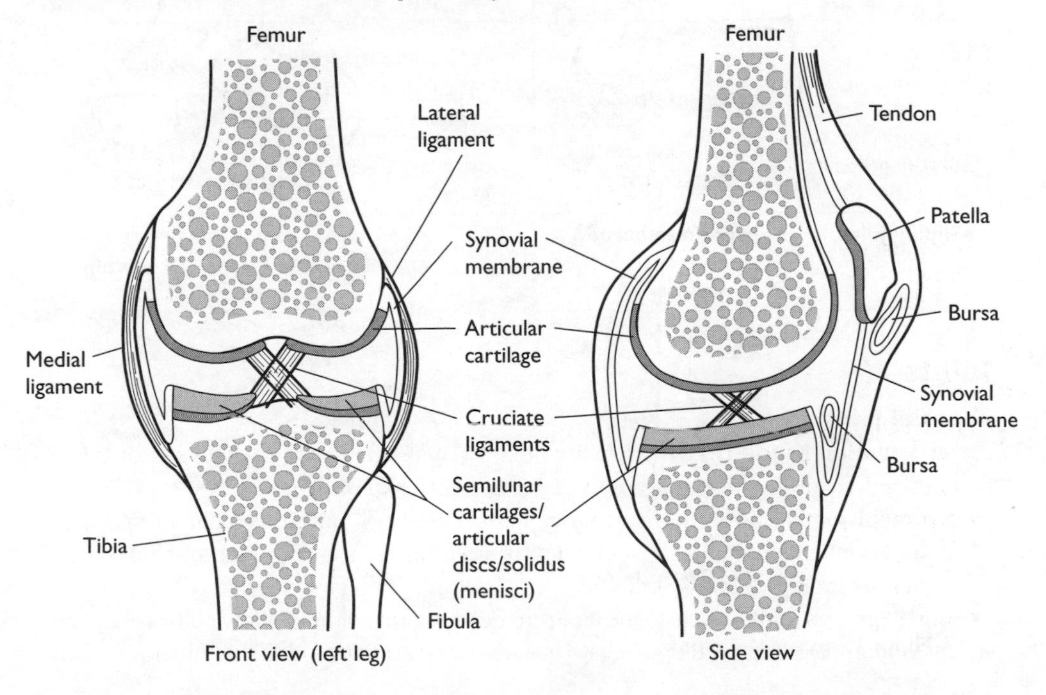

Synovial joints are characterised by the presence of an articular capsule that is lined with a synovial membrane.

The articular surfaces of the bones are covered with **hyaline cartilage**, which protects the bone tissue and helps to reduce friction between the bones.

The **articular capsule** comprises strong, fibrous tissue surrounding the joint. The capsule adds stability to a joint, and stops unwanted material from entering. Capsules are reinforced by ligaments.

The **synovial membrane** lines the inside of the capsule, but does not cover the hyaline cartilage. Its role is to produce **synovial fluid**, which is a yellowish oily fluid that lubricates the articulating surfaces, forms a fluid cushion between surfaces, provides nutrients for the hyaline cartilage and absorbs debris produced by friction between joint surfaces.

Articular discs (**menisci**) lie between the articular surfaces, and are attached to the capsule at the outer edge of the joint. Their function is to absorb shock, maintain joint stability and protect the bone surfaces. **Bursae**, which are closed sacs filled with synovial fluid, are located wherever friction may develop, such as between the tendons and the bones.

Joints and movement

Different types of joint allow movement within specific planes. This is facilitated by synovial fluid and hyaline cartilage, as illustrated in the diagrams below.

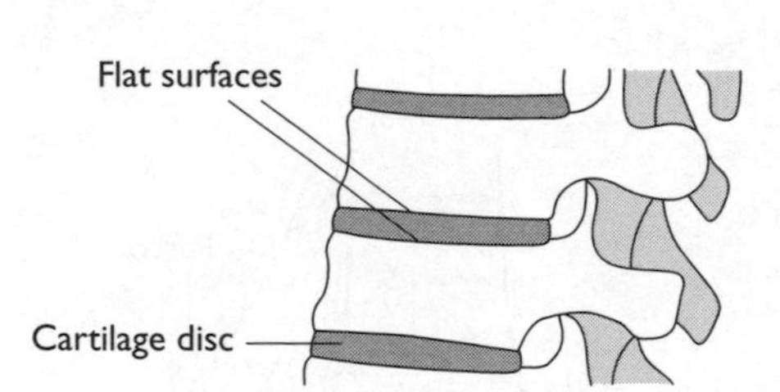

Sliding joint, e.g. between vertebrae

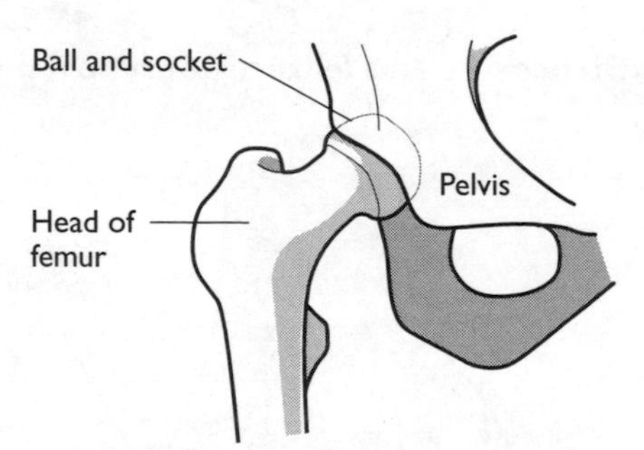

Ball-and-socket joint, e.g. the hip

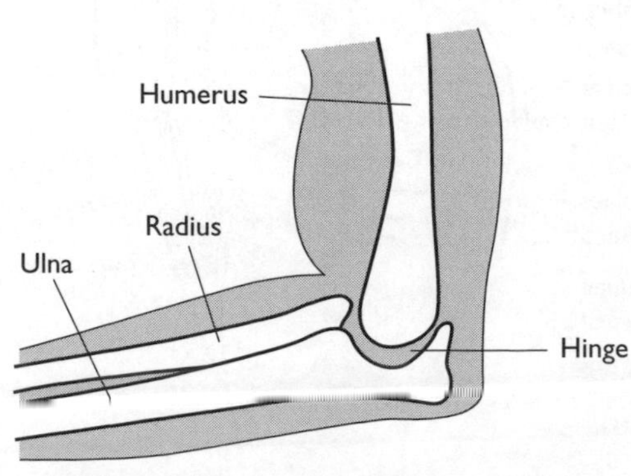

Hinge joint, e.g. the elbow

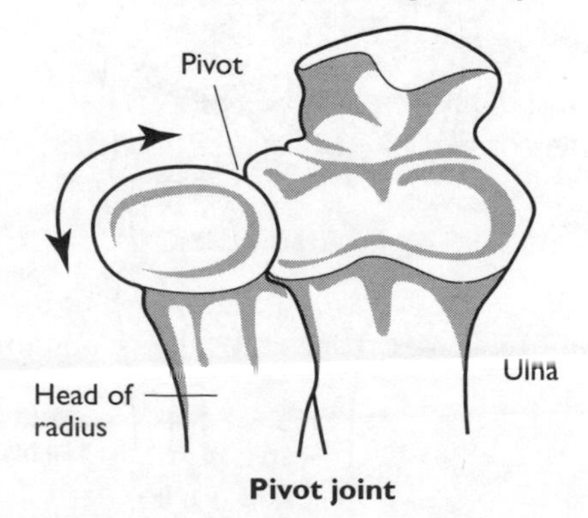

Pivot joint

Bone

Bone is hard connective tissue consisting of calcified bone enclosing softer, even slightly spongy, **cancellous** collagen fibre. Calcium gives the bone rigidity, while the strength comes predominantly from the trabecular structure.

Cartilage

Hyaline or articular cartilage

Hyaline cartilage occurs on the articulating surfaces of bones that form joints. It is bluish in colour and is composed of a network of collagen fibres. The cartilage protects the bone tissue from wear and reduces friction between the articulating bones.

Joint movement improves the nutrient supply to this tissue and encourages growth. Therefore, hyaline cartilage often thickens as a result of exercise.

White fibro-cartilage

White fibro-cartilage is much denser than hyaline cartilage. It is a tough tissue. Its shock-absorption properties mean that it occurs in areas of the body that have to withstand high levels of stress, such as the knee, the intervertebral discs and the hip socket.

Fibro-cartilage

Fibro-cartilage is very strong and 'strap-like'. It fixes bones together in a fused state with no movement. Fibro-cartilage occurs in the sutures that join the cranial bones together.

Posture and postural defects

Correct posture allows the body to function optimally as body parts will be in alignment.

Poor posture occurs when body parts are out of alignment. There are many causes of poor posture — for example, 'lazy posture', poor nutrition, physical defects, lack of exercise, fatigue, emotional factors (shyness), clothing, poorly designed furniture and certain sports. Postural deviations include increased pelvic tilt, decreased pelvic tilt, lordosis, kyphosis, kypholordosis, round shoulders, poke chin, scoliosis, bow legs, knock knees and flat feet.

Hypokinetic disorders can result from a lack of exercise caused by conditions such as coronary heart disease, diabetes, obesity and lower back pain.

Analysis of movement

Our skeletal structure allows us to move, but it is the force generated by contracting muscles that makes movement possible.

The variety of joint types and muscle shapes means that there are numerous different types of movement. Some of these are shown in the diagrams below.

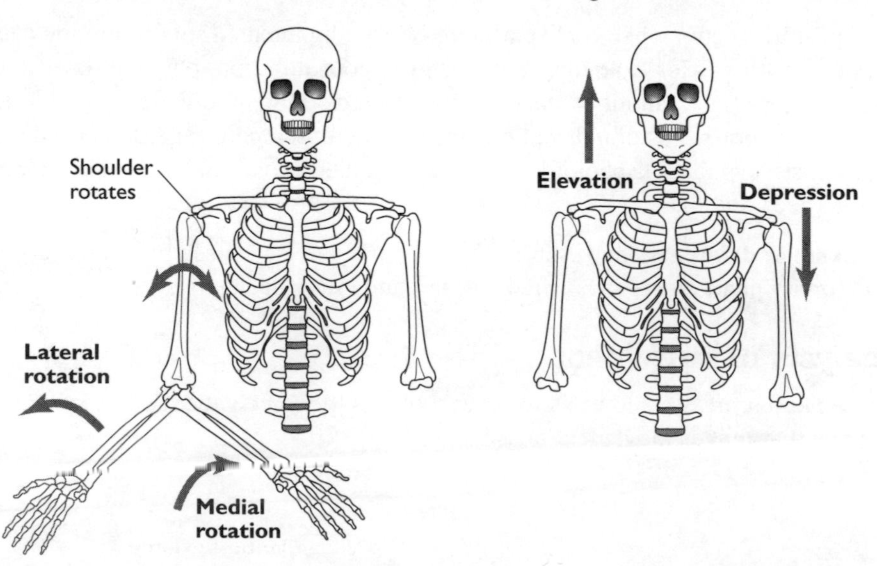

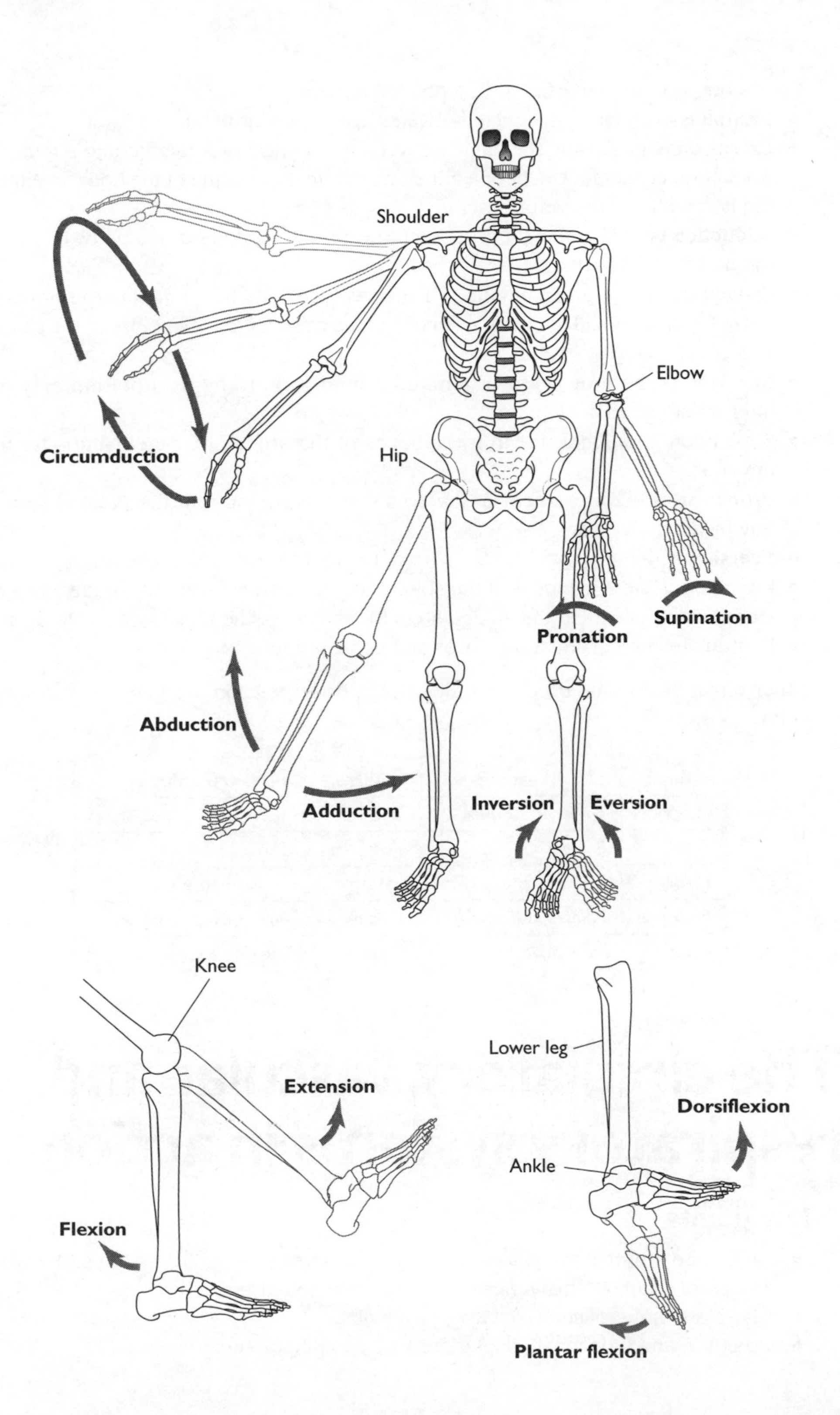
Shoulder
Elbow
Circumduction
Hip
Supination
Pronation
Abduction
Adduction
Inversion
Eversion
Knee
Lower leg
Extension
Dorsiflexion
Ankle
Flexion
Plantar flexion

The following terms are used to describe movements:

- **Flexion** is decreasing the angle between two bones, or bending a joint.
- **Extension** is increasing the angle between two bones, or straightening a joint.
- **Abduction** is the movement of a bone away from the midline of the body, in either the horizontal or the vertical plane.
- **Adduction** is the movement of a bone towards the midline of the body, in either the horizontal or vertical plane.
- **Circumduction** is a combination of the two previous movements. The bone is moved so that its end moves in a circle and the overall movement makes the shape of a cone.
- **Rotation** is the movement of a bone around a central axis. Rotation may be internal or external.
- **Supination** is the movement of the bones of the arm so that the palm is facing upwards.
- **Pronation** is the movement of the bones of the arm so that the palm is facing downwards.
- **Eversion** is the movement of the sole of the foot outward from the ankle.
- **Inversion** is the movement of the sole of the foot inward from the ankle.
- **Dorsiflexion** occurs at the ankle and is the raising of the toes towards the tibia.
- **Plantar flexion** occurs at the ankle and is the pointing of the toes.

Other directional terms used when describing body position are given in the table below.

Term	Meaning	Term	Meaning
Superior	Towards the head	Inferior	Towards the feet
Anterior	Front	Posterior	Back
Medial	Towards the midline	Lateral	Towards the side
Proximal	Nearer the trunk	Distal	Further from the trunk
Prone	Face down	Supine	Face up

The circulatory, vascular and respiratory systems in action

Key points

- Components of the circulatory, vascular and respiratory (CVR) systems, the way they work and how this varies during exercise and at rest.
- Where and how gaseous exchange takes place.
- Structural and functional adaptations of CVR components.

THE HENLEY COLLEGE LIBRARY

- VO_2max and factors that affect it.
- Altitude training and less scrupulous ways of improving aerobic performance.

In summary:

- The **heart** is a muscular organ that operates within the circulatory system and is central to the cardiovascular system.
- The **circulatory system** delivers the cells' requirements and removes their waste products.
- The **cardiovascular system** refers to the ability of the heart, blood vessels and blood to work under stress to deliver the requirements of cells.

Structure of the heart

The heart comprises four chambers, which are made up of a collection of muscles. Two of the chambers are responsible for collecting blood. These are called the atria. The other two chambers are responsible for pumping blood. These are called the ventricles. The heart is divided sagitally by the septum, with an atrium and a ventricle on each side. Both sides of the heart collect and pump blood at the same time, but to different parts of the body — hence the term **dual circulatory system**.

The cardiac cycle

The **cardiac cycle** consists of two phases: **diastole** (relaxing) and **systole** (contracting). As the atria fill with blood — during diastole — the pressure within the atria increases, forcing the **atrioventricular valves** to open. Atrial systole then occurs. This means that the muscle tissue of the atria contracts, forcing the blood into the ventricles. The **semilunar valves** (at the bases of the main arteries) remain closed during atrial systole. Ventricular systole then occurs, during which the muscle tissue of the ventricles contracts. The semilunar valves are forced open. Blood from the right ventricle flows into the **pulmonary artery**; blood from the left ventricle flows into the **aorta**.

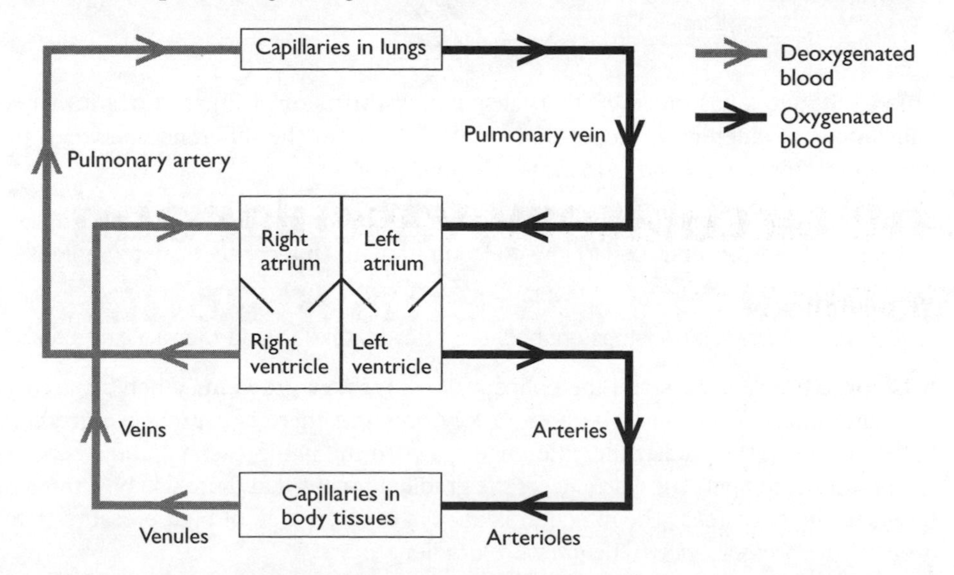

At rest, cardiac diastole lasts 0.5 seconds and cardiac systole lasts 0.3 seconds. During exercise, the length of each diastole is reduced.

Ventilation and gaseous exchange

Gaseous exchange

Gaseous exchange means exchange of gases, i.e. oxygen and carbon dioxide. It takes place:

- between the capillaries and the body tissues
- between the air in the alveoli and the blood in the alveolar capillaries

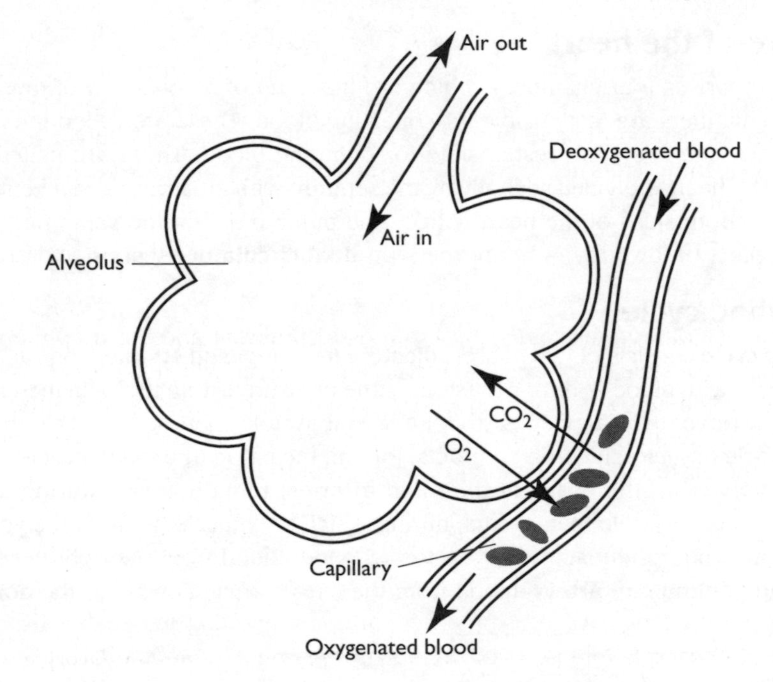

This exchange takes place by a process called **diffusion**. Diffusion occurs when substances of different concentration meet. The bigger the difference between the concentrations, the greater is the rate of diffusion.

Such a difference in concentration is called a **concentration gradient**. Substances always travel from high concentration to low concentration *down* a concentration gradient.

Ventilation

A series of causal relationships enables the body to take in and then to expel air.

It is important to understand the concept of a **pressure gradient**. When an area of high pressure exists near to an area of low pressure there is a **pressure gradient** between them. The greater the difference between the two pressures, the steeper is the pressure gradient. The existence of the gradient means that there will be a transfer between the two areas. The direction is always from an area of high pressure to an area of low pressure, *down* the pressure gradient.

Control of ventilation

The basic rhythm of respiration is governed and coordinated by the **respiratory centre**, situated in the brain.

During inspiration, nerve impulses are generated and sent via the phrenic and intercostal nerves to the inspiratory muscles (external intercostals and diaphragm), causing them to contract, after which the impulses stop and expiration occurs passively by elastic recoil of the lungs.

It is mainly the chemical composition of the blood that influences respiration rates, particularly during exercise. The respiratory centre has a chemosensitive sector, which is sensitive to changes in blood acidity. Chemoreceptors located in the aortic arch and carotid arteries assess the acidity of the blood and, in particular, the relative concentrations of carbon dioxide and oxygen. If there is an increase in the concentration of carbon dioxide in the blood, the chemoreceptors detect this and the respiratory centre sends nerve impulses to the respiratory muscles, which increase the rate of ventilation.

Once blood acidity is lowered, fewer impulses are sent and respiration rate can decrease.

Inspiration

The primary respiratory muscles — the **intercostal muscles** and the **diaphragm** — contract. This causes the chest cavity to increase in volume, which in turn causes the pressure within the lungs to drop. A pressure gradient now exists between the low-pressure area in the lungs and the relatively high-pressure area of the atmosphere. This causes the air to move down the gradient and into the lungs.

Expiration

Relaxation of the intercostal muscles and diaphragm and the **elastic recoil** of the stretched lungs return the thorax to its previous state. This causes an increase in pressure within the lungs. As a result, a new pressure gradient now exists from the lungs to the atmosphere. Air moves down this new gradient, out of the lungs and into the atmosphere. At rest, expiration is largely passive.

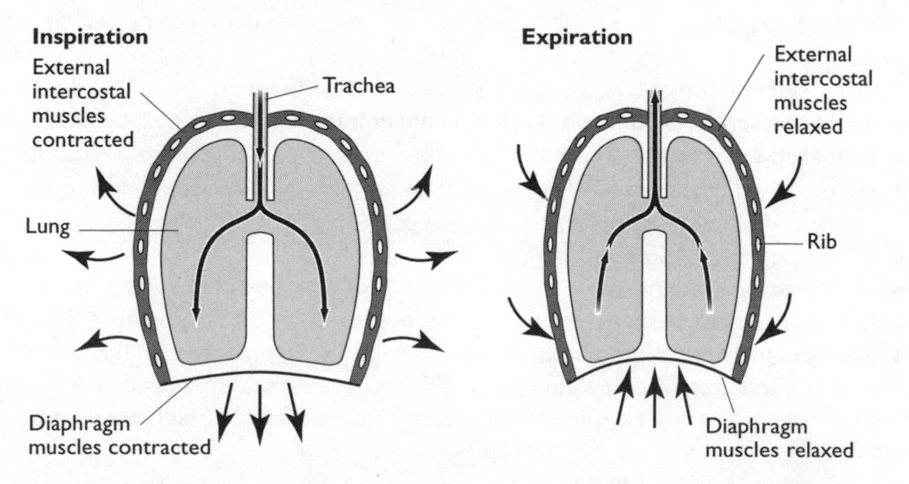

Differences between inspired and expired air

	Inspired (atmospheric) air (%)	Expired air (%)
Oxygen	20.95	16.4
Carbon dioxide	0.04	4.1

Unsurprisingly, expired air contains less oxygen and more carbon dioxide than inspired air. During exercise, these percentages in expired air do not remain constant. As more energy is required during exercise than at rest, the production of carbon dioxide rises as the athlete's work rate increases.

Breathing at rest and during exercise

The mechanics of breathing are largely the same at rest as during exercise. However, the ventilation rate is greater and expiration is more active during exercise.

Breathing at rest	Breathing during exercise
Largely passive	Largely active
Expiration is almost entirely passive	Expiration is more active
Breathing is shallow	Breathing is deeper
Breathing is slow	Breathing is faster
Smaller percentage of expired air is CO_2	Greater percentage of expired air is CO_2
Primary respiratory muscles only used (external intercostals and diaphragm)	Primary and secondary muscles used (internal intercostals, sternocleido-mastoid, trapezius, pectoralis, rectus abdominis)

Structural and functional adaptations to the CVR systems

The effects of exercise

Short-term responses

Short-term responses better enable the systems to meet the demands placed on them. These responses include:

- increased volume of blood ejected per beat (stroke volume)
- increased venous return
- increased heart rate
- increased volume of blood ejected per minute (cardiac output) due to increase in strength of contractions, heart rate and venous return
- increased ventilation rate
- increased rate of diffusion
- increased blood pressure
- vascular shunting — blood is directed to where it is required through a process of vasodilation and vasoconstriction

Long-term adaptations

Long-term adaptations enable the systems to function more efficiently, with less stress to the body, provided the environment remains unchanged. These adaptations include:

- cardiac hypertrophy (increase in size of heart)
- increased thickness of the ventricular myocardium (muscular wall)
- increased strength of ventricular contractions
- increased stroke volume
- increased cardiac output during exercise
- bradycardia (slow heartbeat)
- increased end-diastolic volume and decreased end-systolic volume
- increased parasympathetic nerve activity
- increased red blood cell count and haemoglobin level
- increased alveolar coverage

Structural adaptations (SA) and functional adaptations (FA) are connected.

Exercise results in the heart becoming bigger and stronger (SA). This means that stroke volume is increased (FA). Therefore, the heart does not have to beat as often, particularly at rest (FA). Slow resting heartbeat is called bradycardia.

Arterial elasticity might increase (SA). New capillaries might grow (capillarisation — SA) in parts of the body that require oxygen. Vasodilation and vasoconstriction are quicker and more effective (FA). Consequently, vascular shunting occurs more rapidly (FA) and venous return is faster (FA).

VO_2max and factors affecting it

VO_2max is defined as the maximum amount of oxygen that can be taken in and used by the body per minute per kilogram of body weight.

It is believed that a high VO_2max represents the ability to work at a greater intensity before the body begins to rely predominantly on the anaerobic pathways. Consequently, an athlete with a high VO_2max should be able to work harder and be able to sustain that workload for longer.

Athletes frequently focus their training on:

- improving VO_2max
- achieving their potential VO_2max
- being able to sustain work at a higher percentage of their VO_2max

VO_2max refers to oxygen, so many people take the view that they need to target the system responsible for taking in air, namely the respiratory system. However, several factors indicate that this may not be the best option:

- Approximately 75% of the oxygen inhaled is then exhaled. Therefore, taking in more oxygen may not help — we are not able to use that which we have at present.
- Lung capacity can be only marginally increased.

It is therefore the ability to *use* oxygen that has to be targeted. Many of the necessary adaptations are structural and include:

- increased capillarisation of the lungs, which means there will be more blood available to pick up oxygen
- increased numbers of red blood cells and, therefore, higher haemoglobin levels, which will further enable the blood to carry more oxygen
- increased capillarisation in the working muscles, which will enable more oxygen-rich blood to enter the muscle and speed up the removal of carbon dioxide
- increased levels of myoglobin in the working muscles, which will facilitate greater quantities of oxygen becoming available for energy production
- increased numbers of mitochondria, which will enable the muscles to use the extra available oxygen by the aerobic energy pathway
- fat loss, which will mean that the oxygen will not have to be shared by as much body tissue, making more available for the working muscles

Factors that affect VO_2max

Factors that affect VO_2max include:

- age — with increasing age, the heart and lungs begin to lose elasticity, therefore restricting their working capacities
- gender — in men and women of comparable physical stature, women have more body fat and a smaller heart
- body weight — oxygen needs to reach all living cells, so a larger body requires more oxygen
- activity levels — the more regularly the body is exposed to intense aerobic activity, the more likely it is to adapt and improve its aerobic efficiency

Ways of improving aerobic performance

Athletes try to improve their aerobic fitness to levels greater than their competitors' so that they can work harder, longer and recover more quickly.

Traditional aerobic training will improve an athlete's performance. However, in order to be better than the rest, many athletes have sought other ways to achieve improvement.

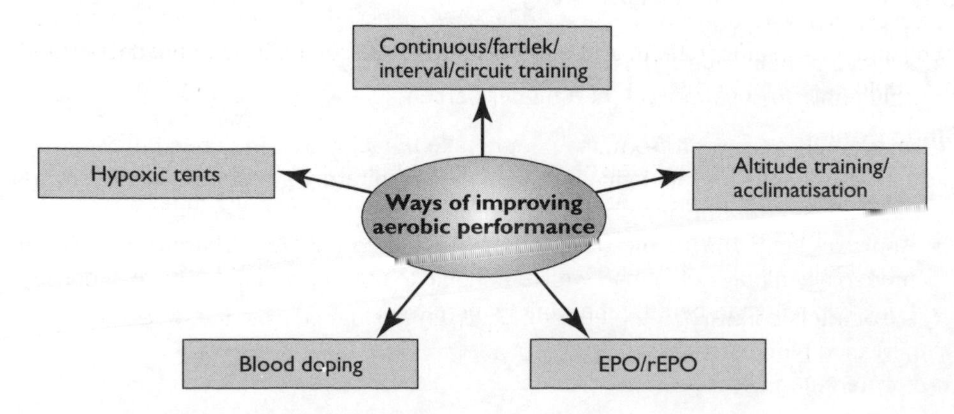

Altitude training

Altitude training is expensive. However, it is probably the most common method used by those who can afford it.

The principle is quite simple. At altitude, atmospheric pressure and the partial pressure of oxygen are lower than at sea level, so there is a lower pressure gradient between the air in the lungs and the atmosphere, and a reduced rate of gaseous diffusion. Consequently, less oxygen arrives at the mitochondria. Therefore, at altitude, an athlete will find it harder to work and train aerobically. The idea is that by training in this environment, the body becomes better able to function with less oxygen, so on returning to a more oxygen-rich environment — sea level — the athlete is able to perform better.

Some points to note

- The sudden increase in altitude leads to a significant drop in aerobic capacity. Therefore, initially, athletes have to reduce their training intensity to compensate.
- The benefits gained may be in part simply due to training intensely in a specific environment — similar to any training camp.
- Oxygen at sea level is of a greater density than at altitude, so the perceived benefits may be lost when the athlete returns to sea level as the body attempts to cope with oxygen of a density greater than at altitude.
- Many athletes are experimenting with training and living at different altitudes — for example, living at sea level and training at altitude (live-low-train-high, LLTH) or living at altitude and training at sea level (LHTL).

Altitude training *must* be undertaken if the athlete is to perform at altitude. This is known as **acclimatisation** to altitude.

Hypoxic tents

The amount of oxygen in the atmosphere inside a hypoxic tent can be manipulated and controlled. Athletes can live, or in extreme cases even train, in them and simulate the effects of living or training at high altitude. The tents facilitate the LLTH method, allowing athletes the opportunity to experience this type of training without having to leave home. After the initial financial outlay, hypoxic tents become economically more attractive than annual altitude trips.

However, there are drawbacks. First, they are expensive. Second, it can feel strange living and/or sleeping in them and many athletes have complained of headaches and interrupted sleep patterns.

Blood doping

Blood doping is an artificial way of increasing the number of blood cells (particularly red blood cells) within the body. This can significantly increase VO_2max. It is carried out by blood transfusion, using either the athlete's own blood (taken 5–6 weeks previously and suitably stored) or matched blood from another person.

Blood doping is contrary to the ethics of sport and is dangerous. It can lead to:

- increased blood viscosity
- elevated blood pressure

- increased risk of heart failure, stroke and thrombosis
- kidney damage
- infection
- circulatory system overload — the direct result of more blood in the circulatory system than there should be, which means that when vascular shunting takes place, blood pressure increases.

EPO and rEPO

EPO is a hormone that stimulates the production of red blood cells in bone marrow. It is a blood protein produced primarily in the kidneys during periods of **hypoxia**. (Hypoxia is a condition in which there is an insufficient supply of oxygen to the respiring muscles.)

Athletes who expose themselves to low-oxygen saturation, for example by altitude training, can experience a six- to nine-fold increase in EPO production. This results in the production of more red blood cells and increases oxygen-carrying capacity.

Some athletes have taken advantage of this by using genetically engineered EPO — rEPO, recombinant erythropoietin — and raising their red blood cell levels artificially. This gives an unfair advantage and is potentially dangerous. It can result in:

- increased blood viscosity
- elevated blood pressure
- an increased risk of heart failure, stroke and thrombosis

Note that rEPO is a banned substance.

Measurement and evaluation of fitness components

Key points

- Reasons for, and timing of, fitness tests.
- Issues regarding the validity, reliability and ethics of testing.
- The names and protocols of tests for each component of fitness.

Issues in testing

Reasons for testing

Fitness testing is undertaken before, during and after completion of a training programme. It provides a great deal of information, which can be used for a number of purposes — for example:

- identifying areas of strength and weakness in the performer
- providing baseline data for monitoring performance
- identifying strengths and weaknesses in training techniques and practices

- assessing the value of different types of training and helping to modify training programmes
- predicting physiological and athletic potential
- drawing comparisons with previous fitness levels and those of other similar athletes
- ascertaining whether an athlete is capable of competing at a particular level
- enhancing motivation
- forming part of the educational process

Issues to consider before testing

There are issues that must be considered before undertaking any type of fitness test:

- The **validity** of the test — are you aware of the specific areas of fitness that you wish to investigate? If so, is the chosen test valid?
- The **protocol** of the test — are you fully aware of how to run the test accurately?
- The **reliability** of the test — for a test to be worthwhile, it *must* be reliable. The athlete must be able to repeat it several times so that comparisons can be made. The athlete and coach must be confident that the only variable that will have an effect on the result of the test is the fitness of the athlete.
- The **current state of the athlete** — is the athlete equipped for the test, both mentally and physically? Has a physical activity readiness questionnaire (PARQ) been completed?
- **Informing the athlete** — is the athlete fully aware of the test that is about to be undertaken, and has consent been given?

Fitness tests

Note: Understanding the various fitness tests assumes knowledge of the different components of fitness and how they are defined (see below and page 40).

Ideally, you should be aware of an appropriate test for each component of fitness. There are many different tests for the various components, and the fitness tests identified here are not exclusive. They are appropriate for the component of fitness in a generic context, but not necessarily for a particular sport.

Appropriate tests for the components of fitness

Maximal strength

Maximal strength is defined as the ability to exert a maximal force once.

Fitness test: 1-rep maximum strength

Protocol: The chosen weight-training exercise is performed for one complete repetition with correct technique and without undue straining.

Cardiovascular endurance

Cardiovascular endurance is the ability of the cardiovascular system to deliver the requirements to, and remove waste from, the body — particularly working muscles — during exercise.

Fitness test: 12-minute Cooper run

Protocol: the athlete runs as far as possible in 12 minutes.

Localised muscular endurance

Localised muscular endurance refers to the ability of a muscle to perform an action repeatedly.

Fitness test: NCF (National Coaching Foundation) abdominal-conditioning test, which requires athletes to perform sit-ups in time to a pre-recorded tape

Protocol: in a bent-leg sit-up position with arms crossed across the chest, the athlete sits up and down in time to the beeps on the tape.

Flexibility

The movement at a joint is determined by joint structure and muscle elasticity.

Fitness test: sit and reach

Protocol: the athlete sits with legs out-stretched in front and the soles of the feet held flat against a vertical surface. Slowly he/she bends forwards and reaches out with both hands, holding the furthest distance possible.

Aerobic capacity

Aerobic capacity is alternatively called aerobic fitness or aerobic power. It is the intensity of work that can be generated aerobically.

Fitness test: NCF multistage shuttle

Protocol: a 20-metre course is marked out. The athlete runs the length of the course in time to a calibrated recording that speeds up throughout the test. When he or she can no longer keep up with the tape the athlete drops out and records the level achieved. The level is cross-referenced to a performance sheet (provided) to give an indication of the athlete's VO_2max.

Anaerobic capacity

Anaerobic capacity is the maximum power that can be generated.

Fitness test: anaerobic capacity test

Protocol: the athlete performs a maximal 30-second bout of exercise (sprint) on a bicycle ergometer that is linked to a microcomputer. During the bout of exercise, the computer records the peak power reached. This relates to the body's explosive power ability and its mean power.

Speed

This is how quickly a body part and/or the whole body can be moved.

Fitness test: 30-metre sprint

Protocol: allowing a rolling start, the time taken to cross a distance of 30 metres is recorded.

Body composition

Body composition refers to the body mass index ratio — the relative percentages of muscle and fat.

Fitness test 1: hydrostatic weighing

Protocol: the amount of water displaced when the whole body is submerged in water is measured. This gives a value for body volume. This is compared with body mass.

Fitness test 2: bioelectrical impedance

Protocol: a small, safe electrical current is passed through the body from wrist to

ankle. Fat restricts the flow of the current, so the greater the current needed, the greater the percentage of body fat.
Fitness test 3: skinfold callipers
Protocol: on the left side of the body, measurements (in mm) are taken at the following sites: biceps, triceps, subscapular and suprailiac. The results are totalled and recorded. The values measured can be compared with a 'norm model' to provide a relative body fat level.

Power

power = strength × speed

Fitness test: sergeant jump
Protocol: First measure the maximal vertical standing reach. The athlete then jumps as high as possible from a standing position. The difference between the reach height and the jump height is recorded. The difference between the two heights is proportional to the power generated, assessed from standard tables.

Agility

Agility is the ability to change the body's direction quickly and effectively while under control.
Fitness test: Illinois agility run
Protocol: beginning from the prone position, the athlete runs around a predetermined course that involves multiple changes in direction.

Dynamic strength

This is the ability to exert significant force repeatedly.
Fitness test: 10-rep max or similar.
Protocol: As for 1-rep max (1RM), but for 10 reps.

Reaction time

This is the time taken to react to a stimulus.
Fitness test: ruler drop
Protocol: A ruler is held, by another person, between the outstretched thumb and first finger of the athlete. Without warning, the ruler is dropped and the athlete attempts to catch it as quickly as possible.

Static balance

Static balance is the ability to support a stationary body mass while not moving.
Fitness test: stork stand
Protocol: Standing on one leg with the sole of the raised foot resting against the lower leg of the balancing leg. The arms can be outstretched for balance, but there should be no movement.

Dynamic balance

This is the ability to support body mass in a controlled manner while moving.
Fitness test: beam walk
Protocol: The athlete walks along a narrow beam. The walk can be performed with a 360° turn mid-way.

Planning fitness and training programmes

Key points

- The principles of training and how to apply them.
- The methods of training and when to utilise them.
- The components of fitness.
- How hard to train.
- How to plan for long-term improvements.

Principles of training

Specificity

Fitness is specific to the type of exercise being performed. Training should involve the muscles and energy systems, together with the skills, needed for a particular sport. For example, strength training develops muscular strength; speed training develops fast-twitch muscle fibres and the anaerobic energy systems for stronger, faster movements.

Progression and overload

Progression

Progress should be visible. It might be indicated by performance or by regular fitness tests and should be further documented in the athlete's training diary.

Progression will take place as a result of a gradual increase in training.

Overload

Adaptations are made by the body as a result of the body systems being stressed. For further adaptations to occur, training must be made harder to stress the systems further. This is the principle of progressive overload and should govern all training exercises.

For improvements to occur, the athlete must train at an intensity greater than his or her existing capacity, so that the training load exceeds that to which the body is accustomed. The result of this will be physiological adaptations to the body. Such improvements generally occur as a result of a sustained period of training over several weeks or months.

The relationship between progression and overload

Although overload and progression are similar and depend upon each other, progression is usually associated with an increase in training *volume* while overload is usually associated with an increase in training *intensity*.

Recovery

This is the anabolic state required by the body so that it can replenish, repair and grow. Only after this phase has been completed will the benefits of training be realised. Training at different intensity levels requires different recovery times.

THE HENLEY COLLEGE LIBRARY

Reversibility

All the physiological adaptations caused by training are reversible if the athlete stops training. For instance, the increase in muscle size (**hypertrophy**), which is a result of strength training, is reversible. If training ceases, the muscle size gradually decreases (**atrophy**). This is a result of the lack of stress to the muscular system.

This principle — sometimes referred to as 'regression' or the 'de-training effect' — is true for all training adaptations, including speed and endurance, as well as strength.

Thresholds

These relate to what is known as the FITT principle. The letters FITT represent:

- **F**requency — how often you train
- **I**ntensity — how hard you train
- **T**ime (duration) — how long a training session lasts
- **T**ype — the method of training used

Over-training

Over-training occurs when the recovery (anabolic) phase has not been completed before the next training session.

Training regimes without sufficient in-built recovery intervals may prove to be harmful, rather than beneficial, to the athlete. They can lead to regression and/or injury. Repeated exhaustive exercise can lead to a depressed immune system, and injuries to joints can occur as a result of muscular fatigue.

Therefore, effective training involves the athlete training at an appropriate intensity and duration, with adequate recovery intervals in the programme.

Over-training can be caused by a lack of rest, poor diet (insufficient proteins or carbohydrates) or over-use of intense or maximal training.

Methods of training

Continuous training

Continuous methods of training work on developing endurance and therefore stress the aerobic energy system. Continuous training involves maintaining the training intensity. Central to this method of training is the performance, at a steady rate or low intensity, of rhythmic exercise that uses the large muscle groups. This should be continued for between 30 minutes and 2 hours.

The health-related benefits of continuous training have been well documented and this, coupled with the fact that little equipment is required in order to participate, has made this method of training one of the most popular among people seeking to improve general health and fitness.

Fartlek (speedplay) training

Fartlek training is often thought of as a modified method of continuous training. It is a form of endurance conditioning in which the aerobic energy system is stressed because of the continuous nature of the exercise. However, unlike continuous training,

the intensity of the activity is varied, so both the aerobic and anaerobic systems are stressed. Fartlek sessions are usually performed with the activity ranging from low-intensity walking to high-intensity sprinting.

This type of training can be individualised. The athlete can determine the speed and intensity of the session. Since both aerobic and anaerobic systems are stressed, a wealth of sportspeople can benefit. It is particularly suited to those activities that involve a mixture of aerobic and anaerobic work, for example field games, such as rugby, hockey and football.

Interval training

This is a method of training in which exercise (work) is interrupted by a period of rest (interval) and then repeated. The training session is arranged around a work-to-rest ratio (W:R). An example of a work-to-rest ratio can be taken from a football match, which has two 45-minute work periods and a 15-minute rest interval. The ratio is written as:

W:R = 45:15 or 3:1

The rest period has to be long enough to enable the body to recover sufficiently to be able to perform the next work period at the desired level of intensity and/or the appropriate length of time. Too little rest will prevent the training session from having the desired effect. The type of energy pathway used and the level of energy depletion experienced determine the amount of rest time needed to replenish the pathway fully.

Circuit training

Circuit training consists of a series of exercises arranged in order and designed to develop general body fitness or specific sport-related fitness and skills.

Fixed-load circuits

Each individual begins a circuit and tries to complete a number of laps or repetitions within a time limit.

Individual-load circuits

For example, each individual is tested on each exercise to find the maximum number of repetitions completed in 1 minute. These repetition numbers are then halved to give the number that must be completed per lap. In each session, each individual performs three laps, trying to improve his or her time.

Advantages of circuit training

The great advantage of circuit training is that it can be used to develop strength, power, local endurance, agility, and both anaerobic and aerobic capacities (depending on the exercises chosen) in a limited time and space. Furthermore, large numbers of participants can be involved.

Overload is achieved in circuit training by:

- reducing target times
- increasing exercise resistance (difficulty of the exercise)
- increasing the number of repetitions

Weight-training

During weight-training, subjects perform a series of resistance exercises designed to develop the fitness component they require in specific sport-related muscles.

Weight-training is a predominantly anaerobic activity, although by varying the intensity and duration of the training sessions it can be manipulated to provide numerous benefits, such as muscular strength, endurance, speed, power, body shaping, fat loss, weight gain or loss, muscle tone and improved posture.

When training with weights, it is usual to target specific muscles, muscle groups or body parts. This might involve:

- isolation exercises — working one specific muscle, e.g. leg extension works the quadriceps
- compound exercises — working muscle groups, e.g. the squat works all the main muscles of the trunk and the lower body

Weight-training should not be confused with weightlifting.

Plyometrics

Power is determined by the force exerted by the muscle (strength) and the speed at which the muscle shortens. It has been established that muscles generate more force in contraction when they have been previously stretched. Plyometrics enables this to happen by taking the muscle through a forced eccentric (lengthening) phase before a powerful concentric (shortening) phase. Exercises that might form part of a plyometrics session include bounding, hopping, leaping, skipping, depth jumps (jumping onto and off boxes), throwing and catching a medicine ball, and press-ups with claps.

Planning to improve

In order to plan an effective training programme, you must:

- decide which components of fitness are needed (analysis of the sport)
- ascertain current levels of fitness against those required (fitness test)
- select the appropriate exercises (methods of training)
- plan when and how to perform the exercises (apply the principles of training)
- review progress (fitness test)

Components of fitness

Fitness means different things to different people. The ability to run for a long time is often the benchmark people use to identify 'how fit they are'. Cardiovascular endurance (which would enable an athlete to run for a long time) is only one component of fitness and is not the definitive component for all athletes.

Fitness is perhaps best defined as being able to meet the specific demands of a particular sporting environment without undue fatigue. There are many different types of sporting environment. This means that the demands placed upon athletes also differ. For example, a shot-putter competes in a very different environment from a 1500-metre swimmer. Consequently, the athletes have different fitness demands and, therefore, place greater importance on different fitness components.

Physical fitness

Some components of physical fitness are given in the table below. Each component is defined and an example of a sport for which it would be important is given.

Component of fitness	Definition	Sport
Strength — maximal	Ability to exert a maximal force once	Weightlifting
Strength — dynamic	Ability to exert a significant force over a short period of time	2000 metre rowing
Localised muscular endurance	Ability to perform repeated muscular action	Cycling (e.g. Tour de France)
Static strength	Ability to exert a force at a fixed point	Crucifix balance in gymnastics
Cardiovascular endurance	Ability of the body to supply the requirements to, and remove waste from, working muscles over an extended period of time	Marathon
Aerobic capacity	Equivalent to aerobic fitness/power and assessed by measuring VO_2max	10 000 metre
Anaerobic capacity	The length of time that maximal intensity can be sustained	Sprint cycling
Flexibility	Movement at a joint	All sports
Speed	How quickly the body or a body part can be moved	Javelin (pulling the throwing arm through)
Body composition — mesomorph	Predisposition to retaining muscle mass	Sprint
Body composition — ectomorph	Tall, with a predisposition to a small body mass	High jump
Body composition — endomorph	Predisposition to storing body fat	Sumo wrestling

Neuromuscular fitness

Some components of neuromuscular fitness are given in the table below. Each component is defined and an example of a sport (or sportsperson) for which it would be important is given.

Component of fitness	Definition	Sport/sportsperson
Power	Strength × speed	Shot put
Reaction time	Time taken to act upon a stimulus	Goalkeeper in hockey or football
Dynamic balance	Controlling the centre of gravity while moving	Beam work in gymnastics
Static balance	Controlling the centre of gravity while stationary	Netball goalkeeper defending a shot

Component of fitness	Definition	Sport/sportsperson
Coordination	Ability to link movements together in sequence	Tennis (e.g. the serve)
Agility	Changing direction at speed and with control	Winger in rugby

Periodisation

Athletes often divide their training year into periods — **periodisation** — using terms such as:

- **macrocycle** — the training period in its entirety. This is usually a calendar year, but for an Olympian it might be a 4-year period.
- **mesocycle** — a period within the macrocycle that might consist of several weeks or even months. There will be a specific objective for this period.
- **microcycle** — an individual training session or small group of sessions (daily and weekly). This is described in terms of the type of exercise performed, its intensity and duration.

Periodisation is a concept associated with recovery from exercise. It refers to the periods that an athlete dedicates to hard training and easier training, so that recovery and adaptation can take place. Periodisation involves a planned training programme in which the year is divided into periods or cycles, often of different durations. Each period has a different purpose. A typical example consists of four periods:

- a preparation period
- a pre-competition period
- a maintenance or competition period
- a transition or recovery period

During the first two periods, training gradually changes from non-specific, general conditioning activities of long duration and short intensity, to more specific, specialised training of short duration and high intensity. Thus, within the pre-competition period there might be a mesocycle for general conditioning, another for strength training and a third for speed work.

The precise duration of the periods and the total length of the complete cycle depend on when the athlete wants to peak. The programme should be designed so that the athlete peaks during the maintenance period, which should coincide with major competitions.

By varying the type of training, periodisation also helps to prevent over-training.

Questions & Answers

This section contains questions similar in style to those you can expect to see in your Unit 3 examination. The limited number of questions means that it is impossible to cover all the topics and question styles, but they should give you an idea of what to expect. The responses shown are real students' answers to the questions.

There are several ways of using this section. You could:

- 'hide' the answers to each question and try the question yourself. It needn't be a memory test — use your notes to see if you can make all the points you ought to make.
- check your answers against the candidates' responses and make an estimate of the likely standard of your response to each question.
- check your answers against the examiner's comments to see if you can appreciate where you might have lost marks.
- check your answers against the terms used in the question — did you *explain* when you were asked to, or did you merely *describe?*

Examiner's comments

All the candidate responses are followed by examiner's comments. These are preceded by the icon e and indicate where credit is due. In the weaker answers, they point out areas for improvement, specific problems and common errors such as lack of clarity, weak or non-existent development, irrelevance, misinterpretation of the question and mistaken meanings of terms. Preceding the candidates' responses are examiner comments outlining the mark scheme for each question, which will help you to decide what to include in your answers.

Training

(a) (i) Explain the benefits of plyometric training and identify the type of athlete most likely to benefit from it. (4 marks)

(ii) Describe a plyometric exercise suitable for an athlete of your choice and identify any potential risks associated with this type of training. (4 marks)

(b) (i) The different types of muscle fibre are sometimes called type I, type IIa and type IIb. Give the alternative name for each type of fibre and identify a sport suited to each one. (3 marks)

(ii) Identify suitable methods of training to develop each fibre and describe the adaptations that should occur. (9 marks)

(c) Training too hard with insufficient rest leads to deterioration in performance. Describe the symptoms likely to be experienced by an athlete who has trained too hard. (5 marks)

Total: 25 marks

(a) (i) There is 1 mark for identifying the correct type of athlete. Any power athlete or athlete requiring muscular strength, power and coordination would be a suitable answer.

There are 3 marks available for three of the following concepts:

- muscles perform a significant eccentric contraction/are forcibly pre-stretched
- provides the potential for a greater concentric contraction, which produces a greater stress and therefore a greater potential for adaptation
- can be made to be very sport specific
- recruitment of type IIa and type IIb fibres

(a) (ii) There is 1 mark for the plyometric exercise chosen, provided it is suitable for the named athlete. There is a maximum of 2 marks available for the description of the exercise and a maximum of 3 marks for the associated risks. For example, for a hockey player:

- bounding and two-footed jumps
- jumping high and landing low with full bend in the knees
- greater load placed on the muscle during the eccentric contraction

However:

- high susceptibility to DOMS
- high susceptibility to joint and/or soft tissue injury
- not suitable for young athletes before physical maturity
- lack of variance/boredom

(b) (i) The alternative name for type I fibres is slow twitch. Any predominantly aerobic-dependent sport would be a suitable answer.

question

Type IIa fibres are also called fast-twitch-oxidative-glycolytic fibres (FOG). Suitable sports are speed-endurance events, e.g. 400 m and 800 m on the track and 200 m in the pool.

Type IIb fibres are called fast-twitch-glycolytic fibres (FTG). Suitable sports are power/anaerobic events, e.g. 100 m sprint and shot put.

(b) (ii) For each type of muscle fibre, there is a maximum of 3 marks from the marking points given below.

For type I (slow-twitch) fibres, continuous, fartlek or interval training would be suitable. The adaptations that should occur include:

- increased myoglobin
- increased density of mitochondria
- increased glycogen stores in muscle
- capillarisation within muscles
- a greater percentage of type I fibres, as a result of type IIa fibres developing slow-twitch characteristics
- being more efficient in aerobic conditions

For type IIa (FOG) fibres, interval, speed, circuit, weight and fartlek training would all be suitable. The adaptations that should occur include:

- increased myoglobin
- increased density of mitochondria
- increased glycogen stores in muscle
- capillarisation within muscles
- increased tolerance of lactic acid
- being more efficient in speed-endurance conditions
- a greater percentage of type IIa fibres, as a result of type IIb fibres developing IIa characteristics

For type IIb (FTG) fibres, interval, speed, weight and circuit training would be suitable. The adaptations that should occur include:

- increased stores of PC (phosphocreatine)
- increased tolerance of lactic acid
- larger muscle bulk
- a greater percentage of type IIb fibres, as a result of type IIa fibres developing type IIb characteristics
- being more efficient in anaerobic conditions

(c) Any five from the following marking points, would score 1 mark each:

- lethargy
- prone to injury or illness
- drop-off in performance
- loss of appetite
- moody
- excessive muscle soreness

- lack of motivation
- weight loss
- reduction in muscle mass

■ ■ ■

Candidates' answers to Question 1

Candidate A

(a) (i) Plyometric training involves bounding or jumping continuously for a short time and then sprinting for a short time. The basic rule is a concentric contraction quickly followed by an eccentric contraction with the aim of improving explosive power. The idea is that the muscles are worked intensively to the point of exhaustion. Consequently they are vulnerable and could not act to protect oneself in an emergency. Because of this, they repair themselves, becoming bigger and stronger so that next time they will be better able to cope with the same intense exercise.

Athletes who benefit from this type of training include 100 m sprinters, because it develops both muscle strength and the power of muscular contractions so that the athletes can compete more effectively in their explosive sport.

e This wordy answer scores 1 mark only — for identifying that a 100 m sprinter would benefit from plyometric training. The explanation of plyometrics scores no marks because the types of contraction are in the wrong order.

Candidate B

(a) (i)
- A high jumper would perform plyometrics.
- It produces a greater stress to the muscle and so encourages a greater improvement.
- An example of plyometrics is jumping off a gymnastics box.
- On landing, the muscles perform a powerful eccentric contraction.
- This then enables the high jumper to perform a bigger concentric contraction on jumping again immediately after landing.

e The candidate uses the example of a high jumper to illustrate understanding of the training. Writing a separate sentence for each point rather than a continuous paragraph is an acceptable way of answering this type of question. Candidate B scores all 4 marks.

Candidate A

(a) (ii) For a 100 m sprinter, plyometric training involving bounding for 20 m, followed by a short sprint of 50 m, would be suitable. This should be done at a high intensity. Plyometric training does carry some potential risks. If the athlete is not fully warmed up, bounding — which should be done as intensively and maximally as possible — carries the risks of muscle strain or hamstring tear.

e This brief description of the exercise (i.e. 'bounding') scores 1 mark, as does the description of the potential risks. Candidate A scores 2 marks.

Candidate B

(a) (ii) High jumper, performing depth jumps.

The athlete starts from the top of a bench and jumps down. During the landing, the muscle groups are working eccentrically and come under extreme force. The athlete then immediately takes off and jumps up, performing a concentric muscle contraction.

The distance reached on the spring could be measured and the athlete could try to improve on that. Alternatively, the athlete could jump over a pole laid horizontally, the height of which is increased over time.

The training could be dangerous and could result in tearing or damaging the quadriceps muscle or the soft tissue in the knee.

e The candidate names and describes the exercise well and identifies the associated potential risks. This is a good answer, scoring all 4 marks.

Candidate A

(b) (i) Type I fibres are more commonly known as slow-twitch muscle fibres. This type of muscle fibre is suited to a long-distance runner because of its resistance to fatigue and ability to work aerobically for a long time.

Type IIa fibres are also known as fast-twitch-oxidative-glycolytic fibres. They are suited to middle-distance runners because of the balance of power and resistance to fatigue.

Type IIb fibres are also known as fast-twitch-glycolytic fibres. They are suited to sprinters because of their powerful contraction and large muscle diameter.

e This is an excellent answer that warrants the full 3 marks. The candidate demonstrates understanding of this area by justifying the choice of sport. The question does not ask for this, but if time permits it can be a useful ploy. In some cases, it might enable an examiner to award a mark that may have been in doubt because of a confused description.

Candidate B

(b) (i) Type I: slow twitch, marathon runners
Type IIa: FOG, 800 m runners
Type IIb: FTG (fast-twitch fibres), 100 m sprinters

e In comparison with Candidate A, Candidate B has provided the absolute minimum required. However, the question has been answered correctly, so the candidate scores 3 marks. This type of answer can save time. However, it runs the risk of perhaps being too brief and so, on occasion, missing marks.

Candidate A

(b) (ii) Weight-training would be a suitable method to use to improve type I muscle fibres. Type I muscle fibres have a low force and speed of contraction. Weight-training will increase the force of contraction and muscle diameter, allowing athletes to have all the aerobic qualities these fibres contain and to have powerful contractions so that they can run, cycle or swim faster.

For type IIa fibres, interval training can be used. This will increase muscle diameter and hopefully, therefore, increase energy stores in the muscles.

Type IIb fibres have great explosive power but can only work maximally for a short time. They are easily fatigued. To develop these muscle fibres, interval training can be used to increase resistance to fatigue and lactic acid build-up.

e Although weight-training can be used for slow-twitch fibres, it is not the most usual method and so to gain a mark Candidate A would need to state that the training would be with a light weight and performed for many repetitions. For type IIa and IIb fibres, Candidate A's answer is too brief for the full mark allocation, but it gains 2 marks in each case, giving a total of 4 marks out of 9.

Candidate B

(b) (ii) Slow-twitch fibres: continuous training will produce an increase in capillarisation and increased aerobic capacity.

Fast-twitch FOG fibres: circuit training will encourage further capillarisation in the muscles. Type IIb and type I fibres will begin to adopt type IIa characteristics.

Fast-twitch FTG fibres: weight-training will increase anaerobic capacity, brought about by increased size of fibres, which means that they will be able to hold larger stores of PC and ATP.

e This is a competent, detailed answer, which is split clearly into three sections. In each section, the candidate identifies the method of training and then refers to the adaptations that are likely to occur. Candidate B scores all 9 marks.

Candidate A

(c) Over-training may lead to deterioration in performance. It is indicated by various symptoms, including rapid weight loss and prolonged lack of appetite. An athlete may experience muscle soreness and have a greater chance of picking up an injury. There may be a lack of motivation to train. All these symptoms are ways in which the body is trying to tell the athlete that he or she is training too much.

e This is a good, succinct answer, which scores all 6 marks.

Candidate B

(c) DOMS — delayed onset muscular soreness. The symptoms are lack of flexibility and sore, tender muscles caused by acid or waste products. DOMS means a decreasing level of performance. It is caused by excessive eccentric contractions.

e Candidate B has misunderstood the question and fails to score.

e **Overall, Candidate A scores 16 marks out of 25, equivalent to a grade B. Candidate B scores 20, which would be a grade A.**

Joints and fitness

(a) The range of motion at a joint is largely determined by its structure and muscle elasticity.

(i) Name and give the location of a synovial joint and identify two types of permitted movement. (3 marks)

(ii) Flexibility training is used to increase the range of motion at a joint. Name and describe two different types of flexibility training used to achieve this improvement. (4 marks)

(b) Identify and define two components of fitness required by a particular athlete, explaining the role of each component for that athlete. (6 marks)

(c) Physiologists such as Karvonen stated that athletes should train in a specific zone in order to achieve particular benefits.

(i) Explain what is meant by the term 'training zones' and suggest how they can be used to aid an athlete's training. (3 marks)

(ii) Identify and describe a suitable method used by athletes to calculate these zones. (5 marks)

(d) Identify a method of training to enhance two named components of fitness. Explain the reasons behind each of your chosen methods. (6 marks)

Total: 27 marks

(a) (i) There is 1 mark for correctly naming *and* locating the joint and 1 mark for each type of movement. For example:

- hinge at the elbow
- flexion
- extension

(a) (ii) The types of flexibility training are:

- static — the muscle is taken to its limit and held under tension
- ballistic — momentum is used to force the fibres to stretch over a greater range
- PNF — the muscle is stretched to its limit and then performs an isometric contraction while stretched; this is repeated after relaxing
- active static — the performer stretches the body part
- passive static — the performer allows a partner to move the limb to the point of stretch

Any two of the above would earn 2 marks each.

(b) There is 1 mark for each component of fitness identified, 1 mark for each correct definition and 1 mark for each explanation. For example, for a high jumper, any two of the following would gain 6 marks:

- Agility, which is the ability to change direction at speed while retaining control. The high jumper must change direction on take-off and also on going over the bar.

- Flexibility, which is the ability to move a joint through its complete range of motion. As the high jumper goes over the bar the back must hyperextend.
- Power, which is strength × speed. On take-off, the athlete must exert a maximal force as quickly as possible.

(c) (i) The marking points are:
- A training zone is a determined work intensity.
- It is governed by heart rate *or* by the ratio of perceived exertion (RPE).
- It enables an athlete to work with greater specificity to the desired outcome.

(c) (ii) Karvonen's theory would earn 1 mark. The remaining 4 marks are for the calculation:

estimated maximum heart rate (MHR) = 220 – age (1 mark)

MHR – resting HR = HR reserve (HRR) (1 mark)

HRR × desired fraction (1 mark) (0.6 in Karvonen's example for aerobic improvement) + RHR (1 mark) = threshold HR

A similar type of description for RPE would also be acceptable.

(d) There is 1 mark for each correctly applied method of training and a maximum of 2 marks for each explanation. Using flexibility and power as the components of fitness as examples:
- For flexibility, interval training for static stretches or specific types of stretch would be acceptable training methods. The reasons are that it enables progression to be made within each interval and increases muscle elasticity, which enables joints to move through a greater range.
- For power, plyometrics would be suitable. It can be very sport specific and it results in a greater positive adaptation (quick results).

■ ■ ■

Candidates' answers to Question 2

Candidate A

(a) (i) An example of a synovial joint is the ball-and-socket joint, which is located in the shoulder. This joint allows rotation, flexion and extension of the arm. Flexion is decreasing the angle between two bones. Extension is increasing the angle at a joint.

e Candidate A scores the full 3 marks. However, the candidate has wasted time by providing information that was not asked for.

Candidate B

(a) (i) Hinge joint; flexion and extension

e This answer is too brief. The candidate has lost a mark for not giving the location of a hinge joint.

Candidate A

(a) (ii) PNF can be used as flexibility training. This involves contracting the muscle before stretching it. This method is used to relax the muscle and allow it to be stretched slightly further each time the stretch is performed.

This is not a particularly well-answered question. The candidate has identified a *single* method of training, when the question clearly asks for different *types*. The description of PNF is vague and confused. Candidate A scores 1 of the available 4 marks.

Candidate B

(a) (ii)
- PNF — taking a muscle to its stretched limit, performing an isometric contraction when at this point — stretch, contract, relax
- Dynamic stretching — taking the joint and muscles through the range of movement likely to be experienced when performing
- Static stretching — taking a muscle to its limit and holding
- Ballistic — using momentum to force a muscle beyond its normal range of movement

This is a very detailed answer which achieves the maximum marks. However, the candidate has ignored the question and wasted time by providing all four modes.

Candidate A

(b) Power (strength × speed) is a component of fitness required by a 100 m sprinter. It is needed for exploding out of the blocks at the start of a race. Speed is needed for sprinting to the finish line and hopefully winning the race. A 100 m sprinter may also need fast reaction times so that when the starting gun is fired he or she is ready to push out of the blocks as quickly as possible to gain an advantage over the other athletes.

This single paragraph means that the examiner has to search to allocate the 5 marks scored. A better layout (for full marks) would have been:
- **For a 100 m sprinter, power is required.**
- **It is defined as strength × speed.**
- **Sprinters need power so that they can explode out of the blocks at the start of a race.**
- **A 100 m sprinter may also need fast reaction times.**
- **This is the time taken from experiencing a stimulus to responding and reacting.**
- **Sprinters need quick reactions so that when the starting gun is fired they are ready to push out of the blocks as quickly as possible to gain an advantage over the other athletes.**

This answer would have scored the full 6 marks. It would also have been clear to the candidate that 6 marks were possible because six points were made.

Candidate B

(b) Javelin thrower

Speed is the ability to put the body or body parts into motion quickly. The run up to the eventual throw needs momentum.

Explosive/maximal strength is the maximum force that can be exerted once only. The throw needs to be the maximum the athlete can produce.

Although it scores quite well (5 marks), the answer is too brief to be awarded the full 6 marks. The answer falls down on the reasons why the athlete requires the components of fitness.

Candidate A

(c) (i) Training zones were first proposed by Karvonen, who suggested that working at different percentage levels of maximum heart rate would result in different adaptations to the body. Training zones can aid training because if athletes are looking at specific areas they wish to improve, they can look at the suggested training zones, work out the heart rate at which they should be working and use this, along with heart-rate monitors during exercise, to achieve the correct results.

This answer scores all 3 marks. However, it includes more detail than is required. Remember that one sentence should make one point.

Candidate B

(c) (i) A training zone is a range of heart rate values you work within.

Candidate B's answer is at the other extreme. It is far too brief and would score 2 marks at the most.

Candidate A

(c) (ii) A suitable method of calculating these zones is to use Karvonen's principle. Maximum heart rate = 220 minus the age of the athlete. The critical threshold is the level at which the body will start experiencing aerobic improvements. This is calculated by adding the resting heart rate (which can be recorded by counting the number of pulses for 1 minute in an artery) to 60% of the maximum heart rate (remember maximum heart rate is 220 minus age) minus the resting heart rate. This is the heart rate that you should reach to be in the critical threshold and begin to experience aerobic improvements.

The examiner is having to search the answer to award marks. Although much of what is written is accurate, and 5 marks are awarded, the candidate seems unsure whether he/she has made enough points to score full marks. A better layout would remove the guesswork and save wasting time.

Candidate B

(c) (ii) Karvonen's principle

This is his belief that at 60% of the maximum heart rate (MHR), athletes will gain aerobic benefit; below this they will not.

He states that:

MHR – RHR = HRR

HRR × % + RHR = THR

(RHR = resting heart rate; HRR = heart rate reserve; THR = threshold heart rate)

This is an excellent answer, scoring all 6 marks.

Candidate A

(d) Power can be improved by plyometric training. This involves an eccentric contraction followed by a concentric contraction while bounding, hopping or jumping. The quick contractions one after the other generate a great force and, therefore, a more powerful movement. This training should be specific. Bounding or hopping using overlong strides is specifically directed at the athlete's legs, which are the most important part for a sprinter. To improve reaction time, various exercises could be used that involve the athlete reacting to a stimulus. Skills training could be used to develop sport-specific components of fitness, such as reaction time.

Again, because the candidate attempts to answer the question in one paragraph, it is hard to ascertain whether all parts of the question have been attempted. A better structure for this answer would be:

- Power can be improved by plyometric training.
- This would involve an eccentric contraction followed by a concentric contraction while bounding, hopping or jumping.
- The quick contractions, one after the other, generate a great force and, therefore, a more powerful movement.
- This training should be specific. Bounding or hopping, using oversized striding, is specifically directed at the athlete's legs, which are the most important parts for a sprinter.
- To improve reaction time, various exercises could be used that involve the athlete reacting to a stimulus. Skills training could be used to develop sport-specific components of fitness, such as reaction time.

Now it can be seen, by both the candidate and the examiner, that the candidate has indeed attempted to provide answers related to two components of fitness — power and reaction time — as requested.

For the answer about power, the candidate scores 3 marks, despite the explanation of plyometrics being rather brief. Indeed, this was not asked for. The answer relating to reaction time is too vague to score.

Candidate B

(d) Plyometric training is relevant to power.

The leaping and bounding involved requires the muscles to contract maximally and quickly, which should improve this component of fitness.

The candidate has been too brief and has only answered half the question. The justification for selecting plyometrics is vague and warrants 1 mark only.

Overall, both candidates score 20 marks out of 27, which equates to a grade A.

THE HENLEY COLLEGE LIBRARY

Fitness training and testing

(a) (i) Fitness tests are often criticised in terms of validity and reliability. Explain these terms. (2 marks)

(ii) Name a type of athlete and identify two components of fitness important for that athlete. Name one fitness test for each component and provide a brief description of the protocol for each test. (8 marks)

(b) Many endurance athletes have used illegal methods to improve their performance. Identify one such method, describe how it works and state the dangers that accompany it. (7 marks)

(c) (i) It is common practice for athletes to divide their year, or even groups of years, into periods. Name this practice and the particular periods used. (4 marks)

(ii) Give an example of how an athlete's training would be adapted in each period. (4 marks)

Total: 25 marks

■ ■ ■

(a) (i) There is 1 mark for a correct explanation of each term. Validity refers to the relevance of the test in terms of what is being tested. Is it specific enough? Reliability refers to whether the test can be repeated within the same environment and produce consistent results.

(a) (ii) For example, a high jumper needs both flexibility and power.

A suitable test for flexibility is sit and reach:

- Sit with both legs outstretched and the soles of the feet flat against a vertical object.
- Reach forwards with both hands, keeping the legs straight and together.
- Measure the distance that can be reached either from or past the feet.

A suitable test for power is the standing sergeant jump:

- Stand with both feet together and measure the maximum reach height.
- From a standing position, jump as high as possible and measure the height reached.
- The difference between the two heights is proportional to the power generated.

1 mark is awarded for each component, 1 mark for each appropriate test and a maximum of 2 marks for each protocol description.

(b) One illegal method of improving performance is blood doping:

- It is an artificial way of increasing the number of red blood cells and therefore the haemoglobin level.
- It is a blood transfusion, using either the athlete's own blood or matched blood from another person.

question

- The athlete's red blood cell count is increased by either removing blood, allowing for natural replenishment and then replacing that which was removed *or* by adding to the existing blood volume using blood from another individual.
- More haemoglobin means the blood has greater oxygen carrying capacity.
- This can significantly increase the VO_2max.

The dangers are:

- infection
- increased blood viscosity
- elevated blood pressure
- increased risk of heart failure, stroke and thrombosis
- possible kidney damage
- circulatory system overload

A maximum of 4 marks are available for the dangers.

Another method is the use of EPO/rEPO (recombinant erythropoietin)

- Recombinant erythropoietin is genetically engineered EPO.
- It artificially raises the red blood cell level and enhances the oxygen carrying capacity of the body.

Dangers of rEPO are:

- increased viscosity of the blood
- elevated blood pressure
- increased risk of heart failure, stroke and thrombosis
- disqualification, if detected

(c) (i) Periodisation:

- macrocycles — main periods
- mesocycles — phases within periods
- microcycles — smaller blocks, such as training sessions or groups of sessions

or

- preparation period
- pre-competition period
- maintenance or competition period
- transition or recovery period

There is 1 mark for the term periodisation and a maximum of 3 marks for the periods.

(c) (ii) Pre-season — the first mesocycle:

- Enables the athlete to ease back into training after the rest period
- Low intensity/technique work/less likely to develop injuries
- Belief that it allows for base aerobic fitness to be developed

Pre-competition period:

- Increase in intensity/development of speed/raising of aerobic capacity/ development of lactate
- Increasing recovery capacity

Competition period:

- Maintenance work/high quality but short duration
- Emphasis on recovery

Recovery period:

- Low intensity and short duration/longer rest period/increased number of rest days/greater variety of activities performed

There is 1 mark for each appropriately described training regime for a given period and a maximum of 2 marks for applied examples in any one period.

Candidates' answers to Question 3

Candidate A

(a) (i) Fitness tests should be valid and reliable so that they are fair and the results can be compared accurately. Validity can be defined as the specificity of the test in terms of what is being tested. For example, there is no point using an NCF multistage shuttle test to test the aerobic capacity of a swimmer because running is not specific to the sport. Reliability is the ability to repeat the test and keep it reliable in terms of the accuracy of the test. For example, if one test for running were carried out on grass on a windy day and another took place inside and the two were compared, the results would not be reliable as external factors affecting the test would affect the results.

This answer scores both available marks. The validity answer is very clear and scores a mark in its own right. The answer to reliability is on the right lines, but it is vague. In this case, although the question does not ask for examples, the example given provides the examiner with the confirmation that the candidate does have a good understanding. The remainder of the answer is unnecessary content. Candidates should *always* provide examples when the question asks for them. They may also choose to provide an example to help explain a difficult concept.

Candidate B

(a) (i) How applicable they are to a specific component of fitness and how accurate the results achieved are.

This would fail to score as the candidate fails to relate the answer to the specific components of the question.

Candidate A

(a) (ii) For a 100 m sprinter, reaction time is an important component of fitness. A fitness test for this is the ruler drop. This involves somebody dropping a ruler from a certain height and the subject reacting as quickly as possible and catching it. The length of ruler that passes before the subject can catch it is recorded. Before the test begins, parameters must be set so that the test is clear: for example, where the ruler is dropped from, how many fingers the subject can use, whether the drop can be seen and so on.

This test is not really valid because it is not sport specific. The reliability of this test can be good, provided the parameters set are recorded and the test is carried out in the same way each time, with no external factors, such as wind.

Another component of fitness that a 100 m sprinter should have is speed. The 30 m sprint test could be used to test this component. Two cones are set 30 m apart and there are acceleration and deceleration areas before and after the cones. The athlete should pass the first cone at maximal speed, so a running start is required. The athlete then sprints the 30 metres without acceleration and the time taken is recorded. The test can be repeated three or four times and an average time calculated.

This test is valid for sprinters because it involves the same exercise as they do in their event — running.

Provided the track and weather conditions are the same (or very similar) each time the test is performed, it is a reliable test.

This answer scores the full 8 marks. Indeed, it could have scored many more had the question asked for the application of the principles of validity and reliability to the tests. However, the question does not ask for that, so these parts of the answer cannot be credited. Candidate A has wasted time by providing this extra information.

Candidate B

(a) (ii) Shot-putter

Maximal strength — 1 rep max test — tests the maximal strength exerted by the performer in one go.

Speed — 30 m sprint test. Two cones separated by 30 m, acceleration and deceleration points. Allowed acceleration beforehand.

This candidate scores 5 of the available 8 marks. Two components of fitness are identified, as is a test for each. However, the candidate offers no description of the protocol for the first test and only a very brief one for the second test.

Candidate A

(b) Blood doping is a method used by some athletes in an attempt to improve performance.

This method involves removing a pint of blood from the athlete. There is then a period that allows the blood to be replaced naturally and then the athlete carries on training vigorously for the event.

Just before the event, the blood — containing red blood cells and, therefore, haemoglobin — that was removed is returned to the athlete's body. Once the blood is back in the body, the amount of oxygen that can be carried by the blood to the muscles, to be turned into energy and used during exercise, is increased. This increases the ability to compete at a higher level.

There are a few problems with this. The extra blood in the body puts the heart and the capillaries under extra stress. This could result in heart problems or, in extreme circumstances, heart failure.

There is also a chance of increasing the viscosity (thickness) of the blood, which could lead to a stroke.

This is a detailed answer that scores the 7 marks available. Reading the answer as given here, it is relatively easy to see where the marks should be awarded, as the candidate has divided the answer into easy-to-follow paragraphs.

Candidate B

(b) Blood doping

This is where an athlete has blood removed after training at a high altitude. The blood is then stored and re-injected shortly before competition in order to improve the aerobic capacity by increasing the number of red blood cells. This increases the amount of haemoglobin in the blood and allows more oxygen to be transported to working muscles.

rEPO

This is a synthetic form of EPO. EPO is produced when the body experiences a lack of oxygen (hypoxia). It is produced in the kidneys and then encourages the bone marrow to make additional red blood cells. This increases the aerobic capacity, because it means that more oxygen can be carried by the blood.

This response shows a good grasp of both blood doping and rEPO. However, the candidate has not answered the question fully. The question asks for the associated dangers, which the candidate has not addressed. The question also asks for *one* method, *not* two. Therefore, the answer relating to rEPO does not score. This answer would score 3 marks.

Candidate A

(c) (i) Athletes commonly divide their year into periods. The name of one full cycle or period is a macrocycle. This is divided into sections called mesocycles, which add together to achieve the aims of the macrocycle. Each mesocycle can be split up into training sessions or groups of training sessions called microcycles. These microcycles taken together fulfil the goals of one mesocycle.

This is a good answer. However, the first sentence 'Athletes commonly divide their year into periods' is not required. It simply repeats part of the question and is, therefore, a waste of time. If the candidate had written the response as a series of separate points, it would have been easy to see that only three points have been made rather than the four required. For example:

- The name of one full cycle or period is a macrocycle.
- This is divided into sections called mesocycles, which add together to achieve the aims of the macrocycle.
- Each mesocycle can be split up into training sessions or groups of training sessions called microcycles. These microcycles taken together fulfil the goals of one mesocycle.

Candidate B

(c) (i) Macrocycle

This is split up into smaller blocks called mesocycles. Each mesocycle is then split into individual sessions called microcycles. This whole process is called periodisation.

e This is a succinct answer, scoring all 4 marks.

Candidate A

(c) (ii) A footballer's training would be adapted in each period by the macrocycle being split into three mesocycles — pre-season, mid-season and end-of-season. In the pre-season mesocycle, the objective would be to achieve fitness levels that are necessary to compete for the season. This could be done by setting up sets of sessions (microcycles), each one concentrating on a different fitness component. In the mid-season mesocycle, the objective would be to maintain the fitness levels of competition. This could be done by various microcycles, each one focusing on a different fitness component. The third mesocycle would be end-of-season and this would allow the body to recover from the season. All three mesocycles add together to make a successful season (macrocycle).

e The candidate identifies the three stages of a footballer's season and indicates that training would be different for each stage because the objective is not the same. It would be easier for both the candidate and the examiner if the work had been set out more systematically, with each sentence relating to a specific point. This scores 3 marks.

Candidate B

(c) (ii) Footballer's season — pre-season, the actual competition and recovery. Each of these blocks is called a mesocycle.

e This one-and-a-half-line answer cannot equate to 4 marks. Indeed, the candidate fails to score.

e **Candidate A scores 23 marks out of 25 — equivalent to a grade A. Candidate B achieves a grade-D score of 12 marks.**

Applied exercise physiology

(a) Athletes can train at altitude in an attempt to boost their athletic performance. Identify a type of athlete for whom this type of training might be of benefit and explain the physiological benefits to be gained. (4 marks)

(b) Define the term *bradycardia* and explain the structural and functional adaptations that enable it to occur. (4 marks)

(c) Define the terms *agonist*, *antagonist*, *fixator* and *synergist*. Using a named sporting example, illustrate each term. (8 marks)

(d) Identify the adaptations to the musculo-skeletal system of an athlete that are likely to occur as a result of prolonged aerobic training. (5 marks)

(e) Describe the main characteristics of fartlek training and explain its suitability for games activities. (4 marks)

Total: 25 marks

e **(a)** There is 1 mark for the correct type of athlete (any athlete likely to make use of oxygen in the energy production process) and 3 marks for the physiological benefits gained.

- Athlete likely to perform at altitude aerobically.
- Oxygen exerts a lower partial pressure at altitude.
- This makes it harder for the body to deliver oxygen to the muscles.
- Consequently, the body adapts and becomes more efficient at using oxygen.
- When returning to an oxygen-rich environment, the athlete should perform better than before.
- Likely adaptations to include:
  – increase in vascularisation
  – increase in stroke volume
  – bradycardia

(b) There is 1 mark for the definition and a maximum of 2 marks for either structural or functional adaptations.

Bradycardia is a low resting heart rate/RHR — below 60 beats per minute.

Structural adaptations:

- hypertrophy of the ventricles
- increased force of ventricular contraction

Functional adaptations:

- an increase in stroke volume
- no increase in cellular size/demand for oxygenated blood — cardiac output remains constant
- the heart has to beat fewer times in order to satisfy demand
- bradycardia will occur when the heart becomes more efficient/better able to satisfy demand

(c) Using the biceps curl as the example:
- agonist — a working muscle that provides movement, e.g. biceps brachii
- antagonist — a passive muscle at a working joint, e.g. triceps
- fixator — a stabilising muscle at the point of origin of the agonist, e.g. deltoid
- synergist — any other stabilising muscle, e.g. the rectus abdominus

(d) Five marks for any of the following.

Muscular adaptations:
- increase in type I characteristics
- increase in myoglobin content
- increase in mitochondrial size/density
- increase in enzyme efficiency
- increase in localised muscular endurance
- decrease in subcutaneous fat levels

Skeletal adaptations:
- laying down of new stress lines/increase in bone density
- increase in ligament strength/elasticity
- increase in tendon strength/elasticity
- increase in production of synovial fluid
- increased thickness of articular cartilage

(e) The marking points are:
- training intensity/terrain varies
- allows longer distances to be covered/durations to be endured
- adaptable and can be used to focus upon different fitness requirements
- incorporates active rest
- reflects the demands of games activities

■ ■ ■

Candidates' answers to Question 4

Candidate A

(a) An athlete who might wish to train at altitude is a long-distance runner. This is because, at altitude, the partial pressure of oxygen is lower than at sea level. This means that the body needs to adapt to the different level of oxygen in order to perform effectively. When training at altitude, an athlete experiences the same adaptations but these happen more quickly, because the athlete can exercise less to get into the same hypoxic state. At altitude, a long-distance runner would experience the aerobic adaptations of increased capillarisation, raised haemoglobin and myoglobin levels and an increase in the size of mitochondria. These adaptations allow the athlete to use more of the oxygen inhaled at altitude effectively and, therefore, to perform better at altitude. When the athlete returns to sea level, where the partial pressure of oxygen is higher, more of this oxygen will be used and so performance should improve.

The candidate scores 3 of the available 4 marks in the first three sentences of this response. However, it is not until the final sentence that the fourth mark is scored. The remainder of the answer is either irrelevant or refers to anatomical adaptations; the question clearly asks for physiological benefits. Although the candidate scores the full 4 marks in this detailed and scientifically accurate paragraph, time has been wasted giving information that is not required. The candidate could have scored 4 marks in just four sentences by answering in the following way:

- An athlete who might wish to train at altitude is a long-distance runner.
- This is because, at altitude, the partial pressure of oxygen is lower than at sea level.
- This means that the body needs to adapt to the different level of oxygen in order to perform effectively.
- When the athlete returns to sea level, where the partial pressure of oxygen is higher, more of the oxygen will be used and so performance should improve.

Candidate B

(a) Endurance athlete, e.g. marathon runner

At altitude, there is a lower partial pressure of oxygen in the air, so the body adapts to working with less oxygen. Therefore, when training back at sea level, the body can then make better use of the oxygen available and can work harder.

Physiological benefits include increased myoglobin, capillarisation and haemoglobin.

This is brief and to the point, and the candidate does enough to score 3 of the 4 marks available. The mark for physiological adaptations cannot be awarded because the candidate has given anatomical adaptations.

Candidate A

(b) Bradycardia is a low heart rate, normally below 60 beats per minute. This may be due to supreme physical conditioning. To allow this, the heart needs to get larger and stronger. This means that the stroke volume increases per beat and heart rate decreases because fewer pumps are needed to pump around the necessary amount of blood.

The candidate does not specify that the low heart rate is at rest, so does not gain the mark for the definition of bradycardia. There are 2 marks available for structural adaptations, but the candidate has not indicated that the adaptations given are structural. Doing so would have ensured that the marks would be awarded. Only one functional adaptation is given but the candidate alludes to a second one at the end of the answer. By setting out the answer more systematically, higher marks could have been gained. This answer scores 3 marks.

Candidate B

(b) Bradycardia means a resting heart rate below 60 beats per minute.

An increase in stroke volume without an increase in cardiac output leads to a drop in heart rate. This gives the athlete a wider range of heart rate values to work between.

Three sentences will rarely score 4 marks. The candidate does not mention any structural adaptations and the information given in the final sentence, despite being accurate and astute, is not asked for in the question. Consequently, Candidate B scores 2 marks only.

Candidate A

(c)
- Agonist — the contracting muscle at an active joint, e.g. the biceps in a biceps curl
- Antagonist — a passive muscle at an active joint, e.g. the triceps during the first lifting part of a biceps curl
- Fixator — the muscle that provides stability at the point of origin of the agonist, e.g. the deltoid in a biceps curl
- Synergist — a muscle that stabilises at any other point in the body, e.g. the abdominal muscles, when performing all exercises

This is a textbook answer, which is clearly structured. It provides four correct definitions, a sporting example for each, and applies the definitions correctly to the examples. Candidate A scores the full 8 marks.

Candidate B

(c) The example used is the biceps curl:
- agonist — contracting muscle at an active joint, e.g. biceps
- antagonist — passive muscle at an active joint, e.g. triceps
- fixator — stabilising muscle at the point of origin, e.g. deltoid
- synergist — stabiliser for point of insertion or any other stabilising muscle, e.g. rectus abdominus

This answer is set out in a way similar to that of Candidate A. Setting out answers in this way will help you to score well on high-mark questions, particularly those that ask for several pieces of information. Candidate B also scores the full 8 marks.

Candidate A

(d) There are many likely adaptations to the musculo-skeletal systems of an athlete as a result of prolonged aerobic training. You would expect the number of capillaries in the muscles to increase so that more blood, and therefore more oxygen, can get into the muscles while they are working, supplying more energy and allowing the muscles to continue working for longer. Cardiac output during exercise would increase. This is because, as a result of aerobic exercise, the heart would become bigger and stronger and, therefore, able to pump out more blood per beat. This would allow it to supply more oxygen to working muscles, more efficiently. This would mean better performance for the athlete. Stroke volume at rest and during exercise would also increase because of a bigger and stronger heart that has the capability to pump more blood and also has greater venous return efficiency. The increase in stroke volume would allow more oxygen to get to muscles and help to increase cardiac output.

This is a poorly answered question, which is let down on many counts. First, it is very wordy. This makes it difficult for the candidate to check that the five required points have been made. Second, it begins with an irrelevant sentence. Third, the candidate does what many others have done in the past when faced with similar questions — namely, making reference to cardiac or circulatory adaptations rather than sticking to musculo-skeletal ones. The question does not ask for an explanation of the benefit of these adaptations to future performance. Candidate A scores 1 mark only, for stating that the number of capillaries in the muscles would increase.

Candidate B

(d)
- There is an increase in the myoglobin content of the muscle.
- There is an increase in capillarisation within the muscle.
- There is an increase in oxygen efficiency as more fibres begin to take on the characteristics of the slow-twitch muscle.
- Tendons increase in strength and elasticity.
- Cartilage is at risk of damage; there is wear and tear to hyaline cartilage.
- Bones might become stronger due to an increase in density.
- Bones are at risk of stress fracture.
- Ligaments increase in strength and show a slight increase in elasticity.

The candidate has listed eight anatomical adaptations to the two systems, which, time permitting, is a good idea. This could compensate for any point that may have inadvertently been repeated or answered in vague terms. The candidate scores comfortably the 5 marks available.

Candidate A

(e) Fartlek (speedplay) training is a type of training in which the athlete changes intensity throughout the duration of the exercise. This allows the athlete to train for long periods of time, changing the intensity to use both the aerobic and anaerobic energy systems. It is suitable for games activities because it can be flexible in terms of fitness benefits. If carried out at varying low intensities, it can improve aerobic capacity. At higher intensities, resistance to lactate can improve. It can be specific to games players because they need differing types of fitness and during games the intensity of exercise changes regularly, so the training prepares them well for this. A defender in football may only need to jog to maintain a good position or mark an opposing player when the team is attacking. However, when the team is defending, the player may have to sprint after the ball.

In its current format, this would score all 4 marks. However, it is unclear how much extra or unnecessary content has been included. Below is the same content with a better structure, making a clearer answer.

- Fartlek (speedplay) training is a type of training in which the intensity changes throughout the duration of the exercise.
- This allows the athlete to train for long periods of time, changing the intensity to use both the aerobic and anaerobic energy systems.

- It is suitable for games activities because it can be flexible in terms of fitness benefits.
- If carried out at varying low intensities, it can improve aerobic capacity. At higher intensities it can improve resistance to lactate.
- All of these factors may be required by a games player.

Candidate B

(e) Fartlek training is training at varying intensity for differing periods of time.

It enables athletes to cope with the varying intensity required, e.g. in football, a defender will often just need to jog around in a match, changing position in relation to the other players. However, the player may have to sprint after a ball for a short time.

Games require different periods of high-intensity and low-intensity activity. Fartlek training caters for both these requirements.

e Because of the way in which the answer has been set out, the examiner is quickly able to ascertain that only three points have been made rather than the four points indicated by the 4-mark allocation. Fartlek training has been defined correctly and its relevance for a games player justified. However, the candidate has not expanded upon the characteristics of fartlek training, as required by the question, and scores 3 marks.

e **Candidate A scores 19 out of 25 marks, and Candidate B scores 21. Both these marks equate to a grade A.**